Praise for
Let Me More of Their Beauty See

In a time when taking the Bible out of context is a popular sport, it is refreshing to read the work of a scholar who is putting it back in! This is the kind of stuff that enlivens the Bible, deepens faith, and sends the charlatans packing.

—Nick Carter
President, Andover Newton Theological School

As a pastor and teacher for more than thirty years, it has been vital for me to help people understand how the context of a Scripture passage deepens our understanding and appreciation of the life of faith. Diane Chen helps us with this task and moves us from a merely personal interpretation to a richer incorporation of the text into the whole of life. By helping us more fully understand the context of Scripture ("attentive listening"), she draws us more deeply into faithful and obedient discipleship.

—Amos Acree, Jr.
Pastor, East Aurora Christian Church (Disciples of Christ)
East Aurora, New York

With scholarly thoroughness Diane Chen provides readers with insight and perspective that brings texts of Scripture to life in fresh and practical ways. *Let Me More of Their Beauty See* is a resource for the pulpit and the pew.

—Brian Henderson
Senior Pastor, Calvary Baptist Church
Denver, Colorado

Smyth & Helwys Publishing, Inc.
6316 Peake Road
Macon, Georgia 31210-3960
1-800-747-3016
©2011 by Smyth & Helwys Publishing
All rights reserved.
Printed in the United States of America.

The paper used in this publication meets the minimum requirements of
American National Standard for Information Sciences—
Permanence of Paper for Printed Library Materials.
ANSI Z39.48–1984. (alk. paper)

Library of Congress Cataloging-in-Publication Data

Chen, Diane G.
Let me More of Their Beauty See: Reading Familiar Verses in Context / by Diane G. Chen.
p. cm.
Includes bibliographical references and index.
ISBN 978-1-57312-564-2 (pbk. : alk. paper)
1. Bible. N.T—Criticism, interpretation, etc.
2. Bible. N.T.—Quotations.
I. Title.
BS2361.3C44 2010
225.6—dc22

2010030554

LET ME

More of Their

BEAUTY SEE

Reading Familiar Verses in Context

Diane G. Chen

Also by Diane G. Chen

God as Father in Luke-Acts

To Deborah Watson

Acknowledgments

My gratitude goes first to Dr. Marianne Meye Thompson, my New Testament professor at Fuller Theological Seminary, who taught me both the importance of not taking a text out of context and the joy of discovery when we do read a text in context. Thanks, Marianne, for all those ah-ha moments, time after time, text after text.

Years later, Dr. Elouise Renich Fraser, my former dean at Palmer Theological Seminary, encouraged me to find my own voice in my writing. Thanks, Elouise, for supporting me in my desire to write for the church audience.

Generous with their time and spirit, Beth Congdon-Martin, Meg McKinley, Debbie Watson, Jeron Frame, and Melody Mazuk read some or all of the chapters in this book. Their valuable feedback vastly improved my drafts. Thank you, each one of you, for your eagle eyes and judicious pencil markings.

I also thank Keith Gammons and Leslie Andres of Smyth & Helwys Publishing. Thank you, Keith, for accepting my book proposal, and Leslie, for shepherding the book through the editing process so efficiently.

Above all, I thank God for his wonderful words of life. Let me more of their beauty see.

Diane G. Chen
Penn Valley, Pennsylvania
Advent 2010

Contents

Introduction

"I lift up my eyes to the hills—from where will my help come? My help comes from the LORD, who made heaven and earth." When you think of the opening verses of Psalm 121, what picture comes to mind? Do you envision rolling hills covered with wildflowers, sheep grazing in the valley below, or jagged snow-capped mountains reaching into a cloudless blue sky?

My first encounter with Psalm 121 came not from the Bible itself but from a scenic wall calendar given out by my church at the end of the year. A beautiful photograph of a faraway place accompanied each verse of the month. Not surprisingly, the first two verses of Psalm 121 appeared under a stunning photograph of the Swiss Alps. Looking at the picture, I marveled at the power of the maker of heaven and earth. I thought to myself, "Surely the God who made these mountains would be able to help me in times of need!"

It never dawned on me that the Hebrew psalmist did not have the Swiss Alps in mind—or, for that matter, the Canadian Rockies or the Patagonian Andes—when he lifted his eyes to the hills. After all, I was eight years old at that time and had never traveled outside of Hong Kong, where I was born. To me, one lofty mountain range was just as good as another; all of them were manifestations of God's creative power. If Yahweh could make mountains, surely he could (and would) protect me if I looked to him for help. The point of the psalm was God's trustworthiness, and the picture of the Swiss Alps in the calendar helped me grasp that truth.

Strictly speaking, my early impression of Psalm 121 was informed not by the psalmist's original intent but by a modern-day association superimposed on the ancient biblical text. If the psalmist was not referring to hills in general, then what did he see? Did he see the hills of the Judean countryside that represented the dwelling place of God on Zion for ancient pilgrims who traveled toward Jerusalem? Or did he think of shrines in high places dedicated to pagan deities and thus declare that his help came neither from the Baals nor the Asherahs, but from Yahweh, the maker of heaven and earth? Either identification of the hills works with the geographical and historical setting of the Israelites, a people committed to worshiping Yahweh while at the same time repeatedly drawn to the false gods of their pagan neighbors. Interestingly, both ultimately lead to the same conclusion: true protection comes only from the God of Israel.

If the outcome is more or less the same no matter how we interpret "hills," why haggle over identifying them, whether they are Zion, pagan high places, Fuji, or Kilimanjaro? Isn't Scripture the living word of God that is accessible to both ancient Israelites and modern-day Christians alike? Doesn't the Holy Spirit guide us in deriving meaning for ourselves when we read the Bible? If the combination of Psalm 121 and the Swiss Alps brings us encouragement and assurance of God's protection, isn't that good enough?

I believe we can gain much more from paying attention to the psalmist's context. Rather than taking away from the effect of the scenic calendar, reading "I lift up my eyes to the hills" with both Mount Zion and the pagan high places in mind adds theological depth and historical texture to the psalm. It allows us to connect the psalmist's reflection with other scriptural images of Zion that point to God's salvation, even as it recalls the consequences of Israel's idolatry and warns us against the futility of worshiping false gods. While the photograph of the Swiss Alps may underscore God's creative power, it fails to express the longing, promise, and fidelity that are essential to a relationship of trust between God and his people. A surface reading of Psalm 121 may not be wrong, but it can leave the text flat and one-dimensional. A contextual reading, however, takes into account the author's point of view and opens an avenue for a deeper understanding. Having thought about Zion and hill deities in relation to this psalm, I can never look at a picture of the Swiss Alps in the same way again.

We tend to feel most confident about the meaning of familiar verses. We commit them to memory and use them as encouragement to others and ourselves in specific situations. I deliberately chose Psalm 121 as an illustration because it is one of the most recognizable psalms. We read it, see it on posters and calendars, and even sing about it. We hike up the mountains, behold the grandeur of the scenic view, and recite with appreciation the opening verses of this psalm. For some people, the association has become just as familiar and automatic as the verses themselves.

We often match Bible verses to specific applications. For comfort, we turn to Romans 8:28: "We know that all things work together for good for those who love God." For evangelism, we appeal to Jesus' words in Revelation 3:20: "Listen! I am standing at the door, knocking." When we need to offer criticism, we draw support from Paul in Ephesians 4:15: "Speak the truth in love." We have become so accustomed to using particular verses in particular ways that we rarely pause to consult the larger section of Scripture surrounding them. We assume that our interpretation of the texts is congruent with their contexts. The question is whether we know this for sure.

Let me be the first to admit that I have been guilty of taking familiar verses for granted, assuming that I know the meaning, and unwittingly misusing each of the New Testament texts discussed in this book. My suspicion is that I am not alone in this. While our interpretive blunders have good intentions, I hope this book will enable us to practice reading Scripture in a way that is contextually sound, in order that something good may turn into something even better.

A contextually sound reading of Scripture is helpful for two reasons. First, even though we believe God speaks to us through his word, we cannot ignore the fact that biblical writers lived in a time and place very different from our own. In the New Testament, which is the focus of this book, each Gospel or letter was written by a historical person for the benefit of a historical Christian community within the first-century Greco-Roman world. When we come to a passage with the worldview and experience of the twenty-first century, we may not detect the allusions and cultural scripts that were common knowledge to the ancient readers. Anything that would have gone without saying for Jewish and Gentile believers in the early church now needs to be spelled out for us.

Second, bridging this cultural and historical gap between the authors and us reflects our view of the nature and function of Scripture. The Bible is not merely a manual for Christian living filled with do's and don'ts, but a set of gathered testimonies that proclaim God's saving actions in the world. We have to beware of an easy slide from the pages of the Bible to our current situation because the writings are culturally and historically conditioned. If we consider ourselves fellow sojourners with the faithful people of God, riding on the trajectory of Israel and the early church and embracing their story as our story, we must strive to read the Bible alongside the ancient authors and readers. From them, we glean insights, guidance, and assurance for our journey of faith today.

This book is about developing good habits in biblical interpretation. It is about building on what we already know and making necessary adjustments to aid our reading of the text. This book is an invitation to revisit familiar passages together. By posing historical and literary questions about each text, I hope to add to your appreciation of it. My hope is that the joy of exploration together will enhance our understanding of familiar passages of Scripture. In doing so, we may find a more vibrant message for our churches today.

At the end of each chapter, I have included questions for discussion and a list of additional readings. The books and journals listed should be easily accessible through a theological library. I hope the questions will help stimulate interesting discussions in small groups and Sunday school classes. Together, let's take a journey to revisit some of our most familiar Bible verses. Welcome aboard!

Chapter 1

Take Up the Cross

Mark 8:34

"We all have our cross to bear." These words, whether from our own lips or from those of another, tend to be spoken with a sense of resignation. They are often accompanied by a long sigh. In day-to-day conversation, we use this idiom to express a duty or an obligation to fulfill a responsibility, carry a burden, or respond to a situation we cannot change. The situation varies from person to person. It may involve taking care of a family member with a long-term illness or a debilitating disease; navigating tensions with an overbearing parent, a wayward child, or an unfaithful spouse; grieving a broken relationship; or feeling trapped in a thankless job with an unreasonable or unethical supervisor. Whether we are talking about our own burdens or lending a sympathetic ear to another going through hard times, at some point in the conversation someone might say, "Yes, we all have our cross to bear." In a few words, we communicate a sense of solidarity. Coping with the "cross" at hand, regardless of its shape or form, is a common experience. The idiom conveys at least this much: should we find ourselves in a challenging situation, even though it is not something we have bargained for, we need to hunker down and carry the load for as long as necessary until the "cross" is lifted.

The determination to stay afloat in the midst of a storm is echoed in the lyrics of quite a few songs by popular artists. I have found at least five with the title "Cross to Bear." For example, Impellitteri opens with "Everybody's got their cross to bear, the cards were dealt, life ain't fair."[1] Billy Joel sings, "We all have our cross to bear. We all walk in darkness sometimes. Though I know it don't seem fair, we all have our cross to bear."[2] Likewise, Vonda Shepard's song has the following refrain: "We all got our cross to bear, our star of David, our dreadlocked hair. And oh, yeah, baby, I still care, and if you need some help, you know I'll always be there."[3] All these artists depict cross-bearing as part of the human predicament. While nobody thinks they deserve to be in these situations in the first place, they find solace in knowing that others bear crosses as well. Misery loves company, the songwriters imply, and it is not a bad thing.

The American Heritage Dictionary of Idioms traces the origin of the expression back to Jesus carrying his cross on the road to Golgotha.[4] This seems to be the case according to the Fourth Gospel (John 19:17), but the other three Gospels report that the soldiers seized Simon of Cyrene and ordered him to carry Jesus' cross (Matt 27:32; Mark 15:21; Luke 23:26). Even so, when we use the idiom "to carry one's cross" today to talk about our difficulties or trials, we may be thinking of Jesus, whether for identification or encouragement, and giving ourselves a little pep talk: "If Jesus could do it, I could (or should be able to) do it too!" Presumably, we have established a point of contact between Jesus and ourselves through suffering.

The link with Jesus, however, needs further qualification. First, not everyone who claims to have a cross to bear cares about Jesus' suffering or is even aware of the religious background behind the idiom. Second, this expression is sometimes used in contexts that are far less dire than those mentioned above, so that even an irritation or an inconvenience may be labeled as a cross to bear. Third, the sense of resignation in the popular usage casts the cross-bearer in the role of a victim crushed by the hand of fate. This role runs counter to Jesus' purposeful and deliberate journey to the cross under the mandate of God. Fourth, while an identification may be made in modern speech between our suffering and Jesus' crucifixion, Jesus' call to his disciples to deny themselves, take up their crosses, and follow him is rarely mentioned (Matt 16:24; Mark 8:34; Luke 9:23). In other words, the emphasis remains on coping with and finding comfort amid suffering rather than on the serious commitment required of discipleship. As a result, the significance and power of the expression "to take up one's cross" is diminished.

Given the discrepancy between the biblical understanding of taking up one's cross and the modern use of the expression "to bear one's cross," it is helpful to revisit the scriptural narratives. There we can clarify the meaning of Jesus' carrying of his cross as well as the call to his followers to take up their crosses and follow him. In this chapter, we focus on the latter, using Mark 8:27-38 as our main text. If we use the idiom and claim that we have our crosses to bear, we need to appreciate the way the disciples (and the ancient Christians for whom the Gospel was originally written) appropriated the words of Jesus in their first-century settings. We will soon realize that "taking up the cross" or "bearing the cross" is not a survival mechanism for whatever happens to us, nor is it merely something to endure with a stiff upper lip. Jesus' demand for obedience and commitment goes beyond persevering through the hardships of daily living, even with the best of attitudes. For Jesus and his disciples, the call to bear a cross includes the possibility of losing their lives for the sake of the gospel.

The Paradox of Mark's Jesus: Authority and Suffering

The Gospel of Mark begins with a title that introduces what the rest of the narrative is about: "The good news of Jesus Christ, the Son of God" (1:1). Right from the start, Mark alerts his readers of Jesus' identity as God's Son and his role as Messiah. Written several decades after the death and resurrection of Jesus, this piece of information should not have come as a surprise to the Christians of the first century, who were already confessing Jesus as Son of God and Messiah. This is, however, not so for the characters in the story itself. The nameless but ever-present crowds around Jesus, the scribes and the Pharisees who oppose him, and the Jewish and Roman authorities who put him on the cross never grasp the significance of Jesus. Even Jesus' twelve disciples struggle to come to a proper understanding of their master's messianic role and mission. This is evidenced by the many accounts of their spiritual dullness and lack of comprehension (4:40-41; 6:49-52; 8:14-21). Yet, as we will see in our study of Mark 8:27-38, who Jesus is and what it means to follow him are closely related. For Mark, unless we understand the cross-shaped path of Jesus, we will not take seriously the cross-shaped discipleship to which he calls his followers. Hence, any discussion on discipleship and on taking up the cross must begin with the distinctive portrait of Jesus we find in Mark.

Jesus begins his Galilean ministry with this proclamation: "The time is fulfilled, and the kingdom of God has come near; repent, and believe in the good news" (1:15). Starting with the next verse, the author takes the readers through a fast-paced, action-filled account of Jesus' ministry from 1:16 to 8:26. There are seven specific healings, three exorcisms, four nature miracles, one raising of a dead person, and various summary statements that attest to Jesus restoring people to physical and spiritual wholeness through many powerful deeds. His teaching is captivating and authoritative. By the time the story arrives at 8:26, the crowds and the disciples are filled with amazement as they try to wrap their minds around who Jesus is. They say things like,

• "What is this? A new teaching—with authority!" (1:27)
• "We have never seen anything like this!" (2:12)

- "Who then is this, that even the wind and the sea obey him?" (4:41)
- "Where did this man get all this? What is this wisdom that has been given to him? What deeds of power are being done by his hands!" (6:2)

Given the curiosity surrounding Jesus' identity, our passage (8:27-38) is pivotal in the narrative where Jesus begins to reveal his identity and explain his mission to his disciples, who still don't grasp his purpose. Between chapters 8 and 10, Jesus predicts his suffering and vindication three times. Every single time, the disciples meet his passion prediction with misunderstanding, giving rise to an opportunity for Jesus to teach them about the meaning and demands of discipleship (8:31-38; 9:30-37; 10:32-45). By using different illustrations to underscore the same point three times, the author makes clear that true disciples of Jesus must be ready to follow in their teacher's footsteps, even though the path to glory and vindication is reached through rejection and suffering.

This truth—the twin concepts of glory and suffering—is difficult to grasp, let alone embrace and embody. Will Jesus ask his disciples to do anything that he is unwilling to do? The remainder of the Gospel proves that he will not. If Jesus challenges his disciples to take up the cross for his sake and for the sake of the gospel, he is the first in line to set an example for them. From chapters 11 through 16, the narrative time almost grinds to a halt as Mark spends one third of his Gospel on the last week of Jesus' life. He recounts Jesus' rejection, arrest, trial, death, and resurrection in extended detail. Coming to the end of the book, the disciples of Jesus, Mark's first-century readers, and later generations of Christians who read this Gospel are all presented with one final question: In light of it all, will you still follow this Jesus (16:7)?

According to Mark, Jesus the powerful and authoritative Messiah is at the same time the rejected and suffering Messiah. With this broad assessment in mind, we will now take a closer look at Mark 8:27-38. Let's move from fine-tuning the disciples' understanding of Jesus' identity to capturing the full intensity of Jesus' call to discipleship.

From Prophet to Suffering Messiah

The question of Jesus' identity was a topic of speculation among the people in Mark 6, but now in chapter 8 Jesus himself broaches the subject on the way to Caesarea Philippi. He asks his disciples, "Who do people say that I am?" (8:27). In reply, the disciples provide the same three guesses they have heard on the street: John the Baptist, Elijah, or one of the prophets (8:28; cf. 6:14-15). These three options indicate that a casual observer would have at least characterized Jesus as a prophet, perhaps because of his message of repentance and his ability to do miracles. Both are reminiscent of Old Testament prophets. Besides, the prophets of old were frequently rejected by their compatriots. Thus, when the people of Nazareth take offense at Jesus, he aligns himself with his predecessors, saying, "Prophets are not without honor, except in their hometown, and among their own kin, and in their own house" (6:4). The specific mention of John the Baptist and Elijah drives home this point. Regarded by the people as a prophet (11:32), John was a recent example of a prophet who lost his life by speaking out against evil (6:17-29). Mark's description of John—dressed in camel's hair and wearing a leather belt—further evokes the memory of Elijah (2 Kgs 1:8), another miracle-performing prophet who found himself the target of Jezebel's murderous threats (1 Kgs 19:1-18).

But there is more. Some strands of Jewish thought expected Elijah to come as God's messenger before the arrival of the messianic age. This came from an interpretation of the words of the prophet Malachi: "Lo, I will send you the prophet Elijah before the great and terrible day of the LORD comes" (Mal 4:5). By adapting Malachi 3:1 in his introduction of John the Baptist—"See, I am sending my messenger ahead of you, who will prepare your way" (1:2)—Mark views the coming of John as the return of Elijah. Jesus further affirms this identification. When responding to his disciples' query about the coming of Elijah, Jesus clearly intends to remind them of John and his death when he says, "Elijah has come, and they did to him whatever they pleased" (9:11-13).

Even though the people wonder if Jesus is John the Baptist brought back to life or Elijah returning for the new age, their speculations about Jesus' identity make sense. The problem is that their musings have not gone far enough. Jesus is more than a prophet with a preparatory or precursory role in anticipation of God's kingdom. He is the Messiah whose coming signals that God's kingdom has already arrived. Therefore, when Jesus asks his disciples the more pointed question, "Who do you say that I am?", Peter's answer, "You are the Messiah" (8:29), hits the nail right on the head.

From a general perspective, Peter is absolutely correct. Mark has already said so at the beginning of his narrative: "The good news of Jesus the Messiah, the Son of God" (1:1). Further down the road, standing trial before the Sanhedrin, Jesus himself answers, "I am," when the high priest asks him,

"Are you the Messiah, the Son of the Blessed One?" (14:61-62). Yet Peter's answer, "You are the Messiah," needs serious qualification. The issue is not whether Jesus is the Messiah. He is—there is no question about that. Rather, the issue is what kind of Messiah he will be. Does the way in which he embodies his messianic identity and mission meet the expectations of Peter and the other disciples?

Up to this point, the disciples have seen the powerful side of the Messiah in action—the healings, the exorcisms, the calming of the storm, the feeding of the thousands, and even the raising of a dead girl. Perhaps they are beginning to wonder about the lofty positions they will get in the kingdom, since they deem themselves to be Jesus' close associates. Perhaps they hope Jesus will exercise his authority over Israel's enemies. They would love to see him chase out the Romans and reestablish the Davidic kingdom to its former glory. Certainly the image of such a victorious, warrior-like, kingly messianic figure would fit with Jewish nationalistic sentiments. No wonder the disciples argue among themselves about status and greatness (9:34). No wonder James and John have the nerve to ask Jesus for the choice seats at his left and right when they arrive at the age of glory (10:37).

Lest the disciples become too elated, fueled by their own aspirations, Jesus steers them back to the stark reality of his messiahship. Here he makes the first of three predictions of his suffering and vindication, that "the Son of Man must undergo great suffering, and be rejected by the elders, the chief priests, and the scribes, and be killed, and after three days rise again" (8:31). In chapters 9 and 10, two more predictions follow: "The Son of Man is to be betrayed into human hands, and they will kill him, and three days after being killed, he will rise again" (9:31); "The Son of Man will be handed over to the chief priests and the scribes, and they will condemn him to death; then they will hand him over to the Gentiles; they will mock him, and spit upon him, and flog him; and after three days he will rise again" (10:33-34). These three predictions share similar vocabulary and themes. They all refer to Jesus as the Son of Man who, after being rejected, tortured, and killed by both the Jewish and Roman authorities, will rise from the dead in three days.

The self-designation of Jesus as "Son of Man" in these predictions is intentional. Earlier in the narrative, Jesus twice refers to himself as the Son of Man who "has authority on earth to forgive sins" (2:10) and who "is Lord even of the Sabbath" (2:28). Both references underscore the authority of Jesus, who makes claim to privileges that belong to God alone. Now in the three passion predictions Jesus speaks of the suffering of the Son of Man.

The characterization of the Son of Man as one who undergoes suffering and is then given authority recalls a nameless figure in Daniel 7. This figure is referred to only by the description, "one like a son of man" (Dan 7:13). Daniel's vision begins with four beasts, that is, four earthly powers that oppressed the people of God. Next comes a scene of judgment in the heavenly court, in which the prophet sees

> one like a son of man coming with the clouds of heaven. And he came to the Ancient of Days and was presented before him. To him was given dominion and glory and kingship, that all peoples, nations, and languages should serve him. His dominion is an everlasting dominion that shall not pass away, and his kingship is one that shall never be destroyed. (Dan 7:13-14)

The son of man from Daniel is a collective representation of the faithful saints of the Most High. These saints suffered oppression under the foreign powers but persevered. Daniel's son of man provides a model for Jesus to speak of his own path to glorification and vindication that must come by way of suffering, faithfulness, and perseverance. As such, it makes sense when later in the Gospel of Mark Jesus uses the same designation to refer to his self-giving death: "The Son of Man came not to be served but to serve, and to give his life a ransom for many" (10:45). On the flip side, Jesus also anticipates his vindication by referring to himself three times as the Son of Man who will come in glory with the clouds of heaven (8:38; 13:26; 14:62).

Given the background in the book of Daniel, the label "Son of Man" means far more than a simple reference to Jesus' humanity. Some view it as a counter emphasis to "Son of God," which refers to Jesus' divinity. But by calling himself "Son of Man" in the passion predictions, Jesus is not saying, "I, a man, a human being, must undergo great suffering." It goes without saying that Jesus dies as an actual human being; he does not need to specify "Son of Man" to make the point. Instead, he uses "Son of Man" to make clear the twin aspects of his messiahship—suffering and persecution on the one hand and vindication and glory on the other. While the allusion to Daniel 7 may not be in view every single time Jesus calls himself "Son of Man" in the four Gospels, this Old Testament backdrop is certainly helpful for understanding what kind of Messiah Jesus really is.

It is striking how closely the details in the passion predictions align with what actually happens to Jesus in the last five chapters of Mark. Biblical scholars debate whether Jesus' predictions of his death mean he knew ahead of time the exact details, or if Mark simply edited Jesus' actual words about his death so that the three predictions recorded in the text fit with the actual events. The truth is probably somewhere in between. Jesus warned his disciples of his impending suffering, and then the actual events shaped the oral and written traditions behind what we read now in the Gospels. More to the point, however, is the contrast between the picture of a suffering Messiah and the nationalistic Messiah Peter and the disciples had in mind.

Not surprisingly, Peter is shocked by Jesus' talk of his death. One can imagine a flurry of thoughts that arise as Peter grapples with what he has heard: "Did I not just hail Jesus as Messiah? He told us not to tell anyone, but certainly he did not refuse the title! If Jesus is Israel's Messiah, how can his own people reject him, especially our religious leaders who know the law and interpret the purposes of God for us? Did God not deliver Israel in the past by defeating our enemies? Shouldn't the Messiah do that too? Why would God send a suffering Messiah who will be killed? God promised to send his agent of salvation to save Israel, but where in the Old Testament is there talk of a suffering Messiah? That cannot and must not happen! It would make Israel a laughingstock among the nations, and we have had enough of that! How about his powerful deeds of healing and exorcism? If even the winds and sea obey him, he certainly can get rid of the Romans! No matter how you put it, a suffering Messiah seems wrong!"

Indeed, from the vantage point of Peter and his fellow disciples, there are many logical reasons not to take Jesus' words at face value. It seems that Peter totally misses the last and most crucial part of the passion prediction, which says that after three days Jesus will rise again. The idea of Jesus' resurrection pales against the unthinkable possibility of a rejected and suffering Messiah, and Peter even rebukes Jesus for it (8:32). If we imagine ourselves as Peter, we might have chided Jesus with words to this effect: "How could you have said something so ridiculous? May it never come to pass! What kind of morbid talk is that? Remember who you are—you are the Messiah! God sends you to be a savior, not a martyr! How do you plan to save Israel if you are dead? This makes no sense!"

Jesus responds to Peter's misguided outburst with a counter rebuke: "Get behind me, Satan! For you are setting your mind not on divine things but on human things" (8:33). These stern words, while addressed to Peter, are also for the other eleven disciples who are probably thinking along the same lines as Peter. The Greek verb *epitimaō* is used elsewhere in Mark where Jesus rebukes unclean spirits (1:25; 3:12; 9:25). Peter's objection to Jesus' suffering is so opposed to God's saving agenda that it almost seems evil. Jesus' rebuke of Peter by calling him "Satan"—"the ruler of the demons" (3:22)—is therefore fitting for the situation. On the human level, we can see why Peter's personal hopes and fears are projected onto Jesus. Peter comes across protective and patronizing. For a split second, he takes over Jesus' role as leader-teacher, thinking he knows what is best for the Messiah. Jesus' command, "Get behind me," puts Peter back in his rightful place as disciple and follower.

How can the suffering and death of God's Messiah qualify as "divine things"? The answer can be appreciated only from a post-resurrection perspective. At this point, Peter and the disciples have to put their faith in Jesus' words based on the person they have come to know. They walk in faith but also in fear. As Mark writes, "They were on the road, going up to Jerusalem, and Jesus was walking ahead of them; they were amazed, and those who followed were afraid" (10:32).

God's plan, however, will prevail over any human doubt, fear, and misunderstanding. The first passion prediction reads, "The Son of Man must undergo great suffering" (8:31). An alternate translation is this: "It is necessary (*dei*) for the Son of Man to undergo great suffering." The Greek verb *dei* connotes a divine necessity. Who says the Son of Man must suffer? God says so. At the Last Supper, when Jesus predicts that his disciples will desert him, he cites the words of the prophet Zechariah, "I will strike the shepherd, and the sheep will be scattered" (14:27; cf. Zech 13:7). Who is the "I" striking the shepherd? It is not the Romans but God himself. Jesus knows it too. Later, he pleads in Gethsemane, "Abba, Father, for you all things are possible; remove this cup from me; yet, not what I want, but what you want" (14:36). The "divine things," expressions of the will of God, govern Jesus' life and the way he lives out his messianic mission. In the next section, we will see that this is also what discipleship is about. Acknowledging Jesus as Messiah is one thing; being able to see Jesus' messianic mission as part of God's intention is another. From this point onward, Jesus' disciples will be schooled more and more in the latter. They must not only understand Jesus' true identity, but also realize its impact on their own lives and futures.

Cross-shaped Discipleship: a Matter of Life and Death

From the private conversation between Jesus and his twelve disciples about his messianic identity and upcoming death, Mark moves into another teaching segment where Jesus speaks to both his disciples and the crowd. We do not know where the crowd comes from or if the setting is entirely new. Despite the awkward transition, it is clear that the call to discipleship that comes next is intended not only for Jesus' close disciples but for all potential followers: "If *anyone* wants to follow after me, let him deny himself and take up his cross and follow me" (8:34).

For the sake of gender inclusiveness, the New Revised Standard Version has Jesus give his challenge in the plural: "If any want to become my followers, let them deny themselves and take up their cross and follow me." I have chosen to retain the third person singular pronoun, "anyone," which is what the verse actually says in the Greek. I think this word emphasizes the responsibility of the individual person to speak for himself or herself in response to Jesus. Surely Jesus has both men and women in mind even though masculine pronouns are used. By phrasing it as "if any want to become my followers," the NRSV has furthermore turned the Greek verb for "follow" into a noun, "followers." This makes the sentence lose its symmetry at the beginning and end: "If anyone wants to follow me (verb) . . . and follow me (verb)." In fact, the final "follow me" is in the present tense. In Greek grammar, the present tense denotes a continuous action. "And follow me" means "and keep on following me" or "and continue to follow me." In the Gospel of Luke, Jesus presents the same idea of continuous following when he challenges his disciples to "take up their cross *daily* and follow [him]" (Luke 9:23). Following conjures up the image of one person walking behind another in constant motion. To stop walking means to stop following. Jesus' invitation is not to a single event; it is a call to embark on a lifelong journey. It is not something to be taken lightly.

The two imperatives—"deny himself and take up his cross"—that stand between the bookends of "follow me" explain the type of following that is in view. Self-denial and cross-bearing work together. We will begin with the image of taking up one's cross and then work backwards to the meaning of denying oneself.

Invented by the Persians, crucifixion was widely used as a death penalty in the ancient world by the Celts, the Greeks, the Romans, and other peoples. At the time of the Roman Empire, crucifixion was a capital punishment reserved for conquered enemies, runaway slaves, dangerous criminals, political insurrectionists, mutinous troops, and the like. Routinely carried out in large numbers, crucifixion served to discourage people from attempting an infraction that might put them on the cross.

Not much discussion on crucifixion is found among ancient literature. Few wanted to write about such a horrible punishment. It was not a subject of conversation among polite company. People would rather not talk about it or have anything to do with it. Among the lower classes, wishing the *crux* on another person was like vulgar swearing. The following descriptions from Seneca (first-century Roman statesman and philosopher) and Josephus (first-century Jewish historian) are enough to make anyone cringe:

> I see crosses there, not just of one kind but made in many different ways: some have their victims with head down to the ground; some impale their private parts; others stretch out their arms on the gibbet. (Seneca, *De consolatione ad Marciam*, 20.3)

> The soldiers, out of the rage and hatred they bore the prisoners, nailed those they caught, in different postures, to the crosses, by way of jest, and their number was so great that there was not enough room for the crosses and not enough crosses for the bodies. (Josephus, *The Jewish War* 5.451)

Victims of crucifixion were subjected to utmost brutality, humiliation, and insult. Soldiers treated them as entertainment, as targets for venting their anger, and as scare tactics to force besieged cities to surrender. The criminals were flogged until their flesh was torn to shreds. Bloodied and weak, yet still alive, they carried the beam of the cross to their place of execution. Paraded through the city and crucified naked along busy thoroughfares for all to see, they died a slow death, hanging in the most unthinkable positions. Their corpses were left for vultures and animals of prey to finish off. In the ancient Mediterranean culture where honor was defended and shame was avoided at all cost, the indignity of a crucified person was often harder to bear than the physical torture itself. The sound, stench, and sight must have been unimaginable. Yet crucifixion was so common that people from the youngest to the oldest were aware of its inhumanity and cruelty.

A realistic view of crucifixion in the ancient world should give us pause next time we look at a medieval painting of Jesus on the cross that shows only a few drops of blood trickling from his forehead and his body modestly covered in appropriate places. The old rugged cross is exactly what the familiar hymn says it is—"an emblem of suffering and shame." If we were to stretch our imaginations to what suffering and shamefulness might look like, that is probably where the cross would belong in the minds and hearts of Jesus and his contemporaries. Paul rightly acknowledges that proclaiming a crucified Christ is "a stumbling block to Jews and foolishness to Gentiles" (1 Cor 1:23). Unbelieving Jews would interpret Jesus' death by crucifixion as a punishment from God, "for anyone hung on a tree is under God's curse" (Deut 21:22-23; cf. Gal 3:11). Unbelieving Gentiles would consider it madness and superstition to worship a crucified criminal as one would a god.

With this backdrop in mind, we ponder anew the words of Jesus in Mark 8:34: "If anyone wants to follow after me, let him deny himself and take up his cross and follow me." Jesus does not mince his words. In the context of the first century, taking up the cross spells a horrific, humiliating death. The New Testament attests to the fact that persecution and death are stark realities for Jesus' followers in the early church, hence the constant call for endurance and faithfulness (2 Cor 6:4; Jas 5:11; Rev 13:10). Even though most Christians throughout the ages have not suffered martyrdom on account of their faith, the standard of discipleship and the level of commitment that Jesus expects of his followers—to be willing to give it all, even their very lives—still hold true. If a disciple does not make that commitment before his life is threatened, it will be too late to begin making that commitment when his life is on the line. In other words, the decision to follow Jesus, according to Mark 8:34, includes being willing to die for Jesus and nothing short of that, even from the start.

Now that we are aware of the full measure of what Jesus means for his follower to take up his cross, we turn to the other imperative, "Let him deny himself." Since both concepts interpret each other, taking up the cross, or giving up one's life, represents the highest form of self-denial. This "upper limit" of Jesus' demand will guide our assessment of the following English translations of "let him deny himself":

- "You must turn from your selfish ways." (New Living Translation)
- "You must forget about yourself." (Contemporary English Version)
- "They must give up the things they want." (New Century Version)
- "He must say no to himself." (New International Reader's Version)
- "He must leave what he himself wants to do." (Worldwide English New Testament)

While all these translations convey a sense of giving something up, some of them sound as though the disciples were called to let go of a bad habit or an addiction. Others take self-denial in the direction of asceticism (the practice of an especially strict form of self-denial). These translations indicate that human desire runs counter to the will of God. They all seem to get at self-denial to some extent, but none of them goes far enough. Self-denial is more than being unselfish or not being self-centered, although it encompasses these attitudes as well. Ultimately, discipleship means giving up self-governance and self-determination, so that everything a disciple owns, from material possessions to his own life, is given to the lordship of the one he follows. Whatever is lost, Jesus promises, will be redeemed many times over. Such is the paradox of discipleship.

Why is following Jesus worth all the sacrifice, even the cost of one's life? Jesus explains the paradox further: "For whoever wants to save his life will lose it, but whoever loses his life for me and for the gospel will save it" (8:35). Both lines point to the same idea, expressed first positively and then negatively. Jesus' saying makes sense when we distinguish between two kinds of lives on both sides of the paradox: present life versus eternal life. Consider the rich man who comes to Jesus asking what it takes to inherit eternal life. When Jesus tells him to let go of his many possessions, he leaves in grief. Trying to save his present life and all the wealth and comfort that come with it, he forfeits the blessing of eternal life (10:17-22). On the contrary, Peter and his companions have left everything—family and livelihood—"for [Jesus'] sake and for the sake of the gospel." Jesus assures them that they will receive "a hundredfold now in this age . . . and in the age to come eternal life" (10:28-30). By losing their lives, they will save them. While the disciples have not yet been persecuted to the point of death, if they do not practice giving up what they have now, they will have trouble rising to the ultimate challenge when the stakes become much higher.

The next two questions further emphasize that the present life is miniscule in value and significance when compared to eternal life. The two questions Jesus poses—"What good is it for a man to gain the whole world, yet forfeit his life? Or what can a man give in exchange for his life?" (8:36-37)—call for the same answer: "Nothing." Both questions are proverbial, though the contrast is usually between a life of material excess and a life that has true meaning. Here Jesus moves the contrast up one notch, so that earthly life, even at its most meaningful, is still incomparable to the value of eternal life. In other words, even the best of this present life is not worth holding on to because eternal life is infinitely superior.

Part of setting one's mind on divine things (8:33), then, is placing one's confidence in God's eternal future that far exceeds what this earthly existence can offer. Alluding again to the "one like a son of man" in Daniel 7:13-14 as in the passion prediction (8:31), Jesus assures his disciples that the days of glory are still ahead. He expects them to persevere until then: "If anyone is ashamed of me and my words in this adulterous and sinful generation, the Son of Man will be ashamed of him when he comes in his Father's glory with the holy angels" (8:38). At the second coming of Jesus, this present age will be no more. Now is the time for the disciples to demonstrate their allegiance to Jesus in a world opposed to God and his saving purposes. May their disloyalty not come back to haunt them, for if they renounce Jesus in this life, the glorified Son of Man will likewise renounce them when he returns for the final judgment.

Therefore, the path of the disciples mirrors to some extent the path of Jesus. Even though the deaths of martyred disciples will never carry the saving ability that belongs to the death of Jesus, the general idea—that life comes by way of death and salvation comes by way of sacrifice—is the same. The passion prediction of Jesus establishes a pattern of suffering and vindication that will characterize his followers' mission. There is no such thing as a wayward follower. This is a contradiction in terms. The disciples must understand the identity and mission of the Messiah before they can appreciate the brand of discipleship to which he calls them. Even as their paths to glory will come by way of suffering, what an eternal glory that will be!

Lest the disciples' hearts grow faint, the transfiguration of Jesus on a high mountain six days later serves as a preview of Jesus' glory (9:1-8). Not only is the radiance of Jesus in the presence of Moses and Elijah an unforgettable sight, but the voice from heaven affirms that Jesus is God's beloved Son, and that Peter, James, and John must listen to him. The transfiguration anticipates Jesus' resurrection and also offers the disciples a glimpse of the full display of Jesus' power and authority at the second coming. The memory of this extraordinary event will become a source of encouragement to the disciples when the decision to follow Jesus boils down to a choice between life and death.

Back to Galilee

The journey of discipleship is peppered with setbacks and blunders. Before we leave this discussion, it is worth making one more sweep across the Gospel of Mark to look at Peter, not as the best disciple by any means, but as the disciple with whom we can identify.

Peter's journey with Jesus opens with great fanfare. In Mark's account, Peter (then referred to as Simon) and his brother Andrew are the first two Jesus calls. In response to Jesus' words, "Follow me and I will make you fish for people," the two brothers "immediately left their nets and followed him" (1:17-18). Thereafter, Mark presents Peter as occupying a special position among the disciples. For example, Jesus heals Peter's mother-in-law (1:29-31), gives him a nickname that means "rock" (3:16), and allows him, together with James and John, to witness the raising of a dead girl and his transfiguration (5:37; 9:2). Then, of course, Peter correctly identifies Jesus as the Messiah (8:29). His comfort level with Jesus, fueled by an outgoing personality, is evidenced in his freedom to come up with outrageous comments, such as rebuking Jesus for talking about his death (8:32) and offering to build three tents on the mountain for Jesus, Moses, and Elijah (9:5). One could imagine Peter feeling confident about his commitment to Jesus.

Peter's commitment is undoubtedly real. He left everything to follow Jesus (10:28). He even takes Jesus' words, "If anyone wants to follow me, he must deny himself and take up his cross" (8:34), to heart, and does not shy away from the possibility of death. On the Mount of Olives, when Jesus predicts that his disciples will forsake him, Peter is the first to contest that charge: "Even though all become deserters, I will not." Even after Jesus further predicts that Peter himself will deny him, Peter continues to promise his loyalty: "Even though I must die with you, I will not deny you" (14:26-31). Little does Peter expect this to be a promise that he cannot keep.

In spite of all good intentions, Peter fails to deny himself for the sake of Jesus. Instead, he denies Jesus three times, not before the ruling council or the powers that be, but in front of a servant girl and several bystanders (14:66-72). While Peter gave up fishing nets and family to follow Jesus, at the moment when it really counts and when taking up the cross is a real possibility, Peter cannot muster the moral strength to fulfill his promise.

There is no mention of Peter in Mark 15; Jesus dies on the cross without a single disciple in view, except for some women looking on from afar (15:40). Had the last reference to Peter in the Gospel of Mark been "he broke down and wept" after the cock crowed for the second time (14:72), the story of Peter would be tragic and hopeless. Thanks to Mark's literary artistry, we see a glimmer of hope on the day of resurrection. While Mark does not include accounts of Jesus appearing to his disciples,[5] he does include one piece of instruction for them. The young man at the empty tomb tells the terrified women, "But go, tell [Jesus'] disciples *and Peter* that he is going ahead of you to Galilee; there you will see him, just as he told you" (16:7; cf. 14:28). The two words "and Peter" signal the possibility of Peter's reinstatement in spite of his failings; they offer Peter a second chance.

The question for Peter, the disciples, and later readers of Mark is this: Jesus is moving along again in front of you. Are you coming?

The rest of the New Testament fills us in on Peter's story. The invitation from Jesus to Peter, "Follow me," is resounded twice at the end of the Gospel of John. Jesus commissions Peter to "feed [his] sheep" and predicts that he will in the end give up his life for Jesus and for the sake of the gospel (John 21:15-22). In the book of Acts, we see Peter transformed, no longer timid, but confidently preaching Jesus as the crucified Messiah and risen Lord before Jews and Gentiles, and defending his obedience to Jesus in front of the authorities (Acts 2:14-40; 3:11–4:22; 5:27-32; 8:14-25; 10:9–11:18). Yet the Spirit-empowered Peter also understands suffering. He repeatedly returns to this theme in his letter to the Christians in Asia Minor (1 Pet 1:6-7; 3:8-18; 4:12-19; 5:6-10). In fact, the last piece of encouragement Peter gives to the churches has to do with the twin themes of suffering and glorification: "And after you have suffered for a little while, the God of all grace, who has called you to his eternal glory in Christ, will himself restore, support, strengthen, and establish you" (1 Pet 5:10). In the end, Peter has learned the true meaning of denying himself and taking up his cross to follow Jesus. He has embodied the call to discipleship well and given up everything, including his own life.

Conclusion

In the ancient world, the cross was a somber reminder of domination, defamation, and death. Like many crosses crudely erected along the most visible roads across the Roman Empire, the cross of Jesus was probably rough with splinters, jagged with old nails, and soaked with blood. Vultures hovered above, waiting for the dying to expire. Onlookers stared from below, curious and cringing, vindictive and fearful. Historically, the cross was a common sight shunned by all.

At the same time, for the past two thousand years the cross has been the central symbol of the Christian faith. The message of the cross was central to Paul's proclamation of the gospel, for which he had given up everything. From his letters to his churches, we note Paul's focus: "May I never boast of anything except the cross of our Lord Jesus Christ, by which the world has been crucified to me, and I to the world" (Gal 6:14); "I decided to know nothing among you except Jesus Christ, and him crucified" (1 Cor 2:2). Paul and Peter were but two of countless disciples who heeded the challenge of Jesus to deny themselves, take up their crosses, and follow him to the loss of their lives. Had Jesus, the one whom they followed, not already "endured the cross for the sake of the joy that was set before him, disregarding its shame, and taken his seat at the right hand of the throne of God" (Heb 12:2), his disciples would not have had the courage to walk their journey of faith. Even if this side of glory is accompanied by suffering, renunciation, and obedience, it is not an easy journey.

Next time we encounter the expression, "we all have our cross to bear," in song or conversation, it may be worth pondering the extent to which the situation at hand matches the gravity of the image. If so, Jesus and his disciples have already modeled for us what it means to take up our crosses in faith, dignity, and hope. If not, and if we find ourselves using the image of cross-bearing too carelessly, we may want to choose a different expression. We must try not to make light of Jesus' call to total commitment. But if we do make that commitment, and veer not to the left and right as we follow Jesus, the eternal blessings that await us will infinitely outweigh our sacrifices in this life.

Discussion Questions

1. When you wear cross jewelry or display a cross in your home, what does it mean to you personally? If a friend or coworker asked you about these symbols of your Christian faith, what would you tell him or her?

2. In this chapter we studied the cross in its historical and cultural context. How does this knowledge affect your understanding of Jesus' challenge to take up the cross and follow him?

3. Not all Christians will die for their faith, and many won't have to sacrifice much. In our relatively "easy" lives of faith, how can we view Jesus' call to self-denial in a healthy and effective way?

4. How would you replace the phrase, "We have our crosses to bear," as many people normally use it? What other expression would suit a person's tough circumstances but not misuse Jesus' call to discipleship?

For Further Reading

Craig A. Evans, *Mark 8:27–16:20* (Word Biblical Commentary 34B; Nashville: Thomas Nelson, 2001).

Martin Hengel, *Crucifixion in the Ancient World and the Folly of the Message of the Cross* (Philadelphia: Fortress, 1977).

Joel Marcus, *Mark 8–16: A New Translation with Introduction and Commentary* (Anchor Yale Bible 27A; New Haven: Yale University Press, 2009).

Matthew L. Skinner, "Denying Self, Bearing a Cross, and Following Jesus: Unpacking the Imperatives of Mark 8:34," *Word & World* 23 (2003): 321–31.

Notes

1. http://www.mp3lyrics.org/i/impellitteri/cross-to-bear/

2. http://www.mp3lyrics.org/b/billy-joel/cross/

3. http://www.mp3lyrics.org/v/vonda-shepard/cross/

4. http://dictionary.reference.com/browse/cross to bear

5. Here I concur with most New Testament scholars that the original manuscript of Mark ends at 16:8, and that the verses that follow are later scribal additions.

Chapter 2

Worship in Spirit and Truth

John 4:23-24

It is not uncommon to hear a pastor or worship leader pray, "Lord, help us worship you today in spirit and in truth." To many of us in the pews, this may mean we are asking God to help us come before him with sincerity and a proper attitude. Since not all of us step into church every Sunday fully prepared spiritually, mentally, or emotionally, it makes sense to ask God's help in fostering a meaningful experience of worship. We echo this prayer with our sincere "Amen!" The question is whether "worship in spirit and in truth" really means what we assume it means. Or do we use it because it sounds like the appropriate thing to pray for in our Sunday opening prayer? Some of us are so used to it that we gloss over its original context.

Jesus uses this phrase in his conversation with the Samaritan woman at the well in the Gospel of John. In order to set it in context, we need to consider the story of Jesus' encounter with this woman as a whole rather than highlighting more dramatic or interesting portions. Before we move into the story itself, however, let's raise two matters of interpretation to illustrate that there is more to the passage than what is apparent on the surface.

First, even with the phrase, "worship in spirit and in truth," there is uncertainty in translation. Consider these different English translations:

- "God is spirit, and those who worship him must worship in spirit and truth." (NRSV)
- "God is spirit, and his worshipers must worship in spirit and in truth." (NIV)
- "God is Spirit: and those who worship him must worship him in spirit and in truth." (NKJV)

In the Greek, only one preposition, "in," governs the nouns translated "spirit" and "truth," not two. Also, because the rule of capitalization that we use in the English Bible is not reflected in the Greek manuscript, the word *pneuma* can refer either to spirit in the lowercase ("spirit"—the human spirit) or in the uppercase ("Spirit"—the Holy Spirit). These alternatives allow for various ways to translate the Greek into English, such as, "in Spirit and truth," "in spirit and in truth," or "in a truthful spirit." What kind of spirit/Spirit is in view here—our human spirit or God's Spirit? What is the sense of the word "truth"? Does it mean worship that is an objective reality and not imagined or faked, or worship practiced with honest intentionality and sincerity? Put differently, is this type of worship a matter of human ability, or is it accomplished by the power of God? Given the range of possible meanings, we might wonder exactly what we're praying for. In the rest of this chapter, I will make a case for the translation, "worship in Spirit and truth." I find this one most fitting with the overall context of the Gospel of John.

A second issue of interpretation is whether there is a discrepancy between the author's original points in this story and our focus when we study the passage. Frequently, in a sermon or a group Bible study, we give much attention to the Samaritan woman's sordid past. In the text, neither Jesus nor the author appears to condemn the woman. The precise details of her marital history are not given. While we want to know, we are on more solid ground when we focus on the information given in the text rather than letting our imaginations and judgments run wild. The signature trait in Jesus' public ministry is compassion, and it certainly finds expression in this story. There is, however, a bigger theme than the fact that Jesus goes out of his way to bring the good news to an outcast. This passage is more about who Jesus is than what Jesus does on behalf of the woman.

When we approach the story with Jesus' identity in mind, we put the person and mission of Jesus in the foreground. Viewing it this way informs every part of the conversation he has with the woman. As provider of living water, Jesus mediates the gift of eternal life and the gift of the Holy Spirit. As Messiah and Savior of the world, Jesus is the object of true worship.

Since modern readers are not always aware of the cultural currents in this encounter, it is important to lay some groundwork before we identify the key themes of the passage. Political, gender, and class issues give the story texture. We turn to these now, followed by considerations of thematic elements that the author begins to develop in the earlier chapters leading up to John 4.

Politics, Gender, Class

A thirsty person asking another for a drink is ordinary. Yet nothing about Jesus' meeting with the Samaritan woman is ordinary. Under normal circumstances, a Jewish rabbi would never be caught speaking in public to a Samaritan woman of questionable reputation. If he did, then in one action he would have broken carefully guarded political, gender, and class boundaries.

The history of conflict between Jews and Samaritans is well documented in the Gospels and other Jewish literature of the time. The woman herself points to this separation: "How is it that you, a Jew, ask a drink of me, a woman of Samaria?" The author explains, "Jews do not share things in common with Samaritans" (4:9). In the Gospel of Luke, the Samaritan who comes to the aid of an injured Jewish man and the Samaritan leper who returns to thank Jesus are unexpected exemplars (Luke 10:36-37; 17:16-19). More often, the dislike between Jews and Samaritans is mutual. This is evident in the small vignette where James and John ask Jesus to rain down fire on the Samaritan village that has not shown them hospitality (Luke 9:52-55).

The enmity between the two peoples goes much deeper than surface irritations. The Samaritans are of mixed heritage; they are descendants from the Israelites who intermarried with the foreigners resettled on their land by the Assyrians after the fall of the northern kingdom. Even though Jews and Samaritans worship the same God, Samaritans set up their sanctuary on Mount Gerizim and accept only the five books of Moses as Scripture. In his work, *Jewish Antiquities*, Josephus, a first-century Jewish historian, gives us several accounts of conflicts between the two groups (*Ant.* 18.29; 20.118-136). In 128 BC, John Hyrcanus, the Hasmonean ruler of the Jews, destroyed the Samaritans' temple. On another occasion, some Samaritans defiled the Jerusalem temple during Passover by throwing human bones into the temple precincts, forcing the priests to evacuate the entire temple during a pilgrimage feast. These major clashes happened at each other's temples. This is especially interesting for our story, since the woman broaches the subject of the proper place of worship with Jesus.

To the Jews, Samaritans are no better than Gentiles. In Jewish literature, they are called foolish by Ben Sira, the Jewish wisdom teacher, and assumed to be in a state of uncleanness by the rabbis (Sir 50:25-26; *m. Nid.* 4:1). If Jesus took a drink of water from the woman, he would become unclean by touching the vessel she offered. It's no wonder that even the woman is surprised when he asks her for a drink. Why would a law-abiding Jew flaunt purity laws in such a careless manner?

Yet we know Jesus deliberately chooses to cross the woman's path. This is obvious even before he arrives at the well. While Samaria is situated between Judea and Galilee, it is not the only northbound route available to travelers. It is a faster route, but usually not the preferred one. When the author indicates that Jesus "had to go through Samaria" (4:4), he suggests that Jesus made a specific choice rather than going because he had no other way. In the Gospel of John, the Son is shown to take action only as directed by the Father (5:19). Crossing the ethnic boundary is part of Jesus' mission. While "salvation is from the Jews" (4:22), Jesus is ultimately the "Savior of the world" (4:42).

Because gender relationships in the ancient world were restrictive, Jesus' public interaction with a woman who was not his wife would have raised eyebrows and fueled speculation. Since Jesus started the conversation, a passerby, or even the woman herself, might have thought he extended some sexual overture. The woman, by carrying on a conversation with Jesus, would have also been viewed as guilty by association.

The setting at the well does nothing to clear up the misunderstanding. It might even send the wrong signals to the reader, who is reminded of the betrothal stories of Isaac (with Abraham's servant Eliezer as intermediary), Jacob, and Moses. All these stories took place at a well that involved a drink of water. They, however, differ from Jesus' encounter here, for they resulted in an arrangement for marriage (cf. Gen 24:1-16; 29:1-14; Exod 2:15-22). Perhaps the author finds the location important to the woman's marital history. Jesus does not offer to take her hand in marriage, a gesture that would have meant life, support, and sustenance to her. Instead, he gives a better gift—the gift of eternal life that will forever quench her spiritual thirst.

In addition to race and gender, there is another gap in social standing between Jesus and the woman. Even though Jesus is not a member of the religious elite, he is at least a teacher with a following. By contrast, the woman appears to be hiding from her own people. Otherwise, why does she pick the hottest time of the day to draw water when no one else is around? It allows her to avoid the village women who come to the well early in the morning and late in the afternoon for water and the latest local gossip.

The woman's social position in the village depends on how others assess her moral standing. The text indicates that she has had five husbands, and the one she lives with now is not her husband. Jesus fills in this detail in response to her unclear statement, "I have no husband" (4:17-18). Beyond that, we know little else. Yet we somehow assume that this woman has neither moral value nor respect for her own body, prostituting herself from man to man. We cast judgments: "No wonder she has to hide from the villagers. She's too ashamed to face them. Other women don't want to be around her either. She might go after their husbands! She is defensive and tries to change the subject on Jesus, who shows her compassion." None of those involved—Jesus, the woman, or the author—addresses the cause of the woman's predicament. Her marital history and living situation are what they are. The narrative implies the effect this has on her place in the community. Indeed, she is an outcast with a reputation; the Samaritan villagers do not seem shocked when she tells them that Jesus has told her everything she has ever done (4:28-29, 39). Beyond that, we know little of her past. But she is unnamed, and this somehow makes it easier for us to call her unworthy and promiscuous.

In our attempt to fill in the blanks and make the story come alive, have we exhausted all the possibilities that might have led to her situation? Thinking about this is more than a mental exercise or a feminist effort to redeem her. Instead, it provides a transition from husbands to prophet to worship that has nothing to do with the woman being embarrassed and trying to change the subject.

Five marriages are a lot even according to modern standards. In ancient Judaism, the law allowed for three. Moreover, a woman had few options. She did not have the right to issue a certificate of divorce, while a man could send his wife away for almost any reason, from infidelity to dissatisfaction over a meal. This woman could have been rejected time after time for no fault of her own. Her ex-husbands could have sent her away because she was barren. Or each of them could have died. She could have been widowed and then trapped in the ancient system of levirate marriage, in which the next of kin—the kinsman redeemer—took the widow as his wife so that she could bear children for the deceased relative.

The track record of five marriages could have resulted from any of the above scenarios. This should make us question a sweeping condemnation of the woman's moral character. It may be more appropriate to describe her life story as tragic rather than immoral. Her current living arrangement may not be her choice either. With every divorce, she is older and less eligible for remarriage. The man she now lives with has the advantage of a woman without the legal responsibilities of marriage. But for her, being with him is a matter of survival. Even if her predicament is her fault, Jesus meets her where she is. He recognizes that her need runs much deeper than water for drinking, cooking, and bathing. She needs life, and he is the only one with the power to give it.

Because of the religious, political, gender, and class barriers between them, Jesus and the Samaritan woman have an extraordinary encounter by any standard. No wonder the disciples are shocked to see them together and too uncomfortable to challenge Jesus' action (4:27). Ironically, the story that begins with nothing right about it moves toward an ending that summarizes the saving agenda of God. To appreciate this movement, we need to get familiar with some of the key themes the author develops in the first three chapters of John.

Themes in John 1–3

In the prologue of John (1:1-18), the author lays out the divine and human identities of Jesus: the divine Word was in the presence of God at creation; the Word was the mediator of life who became flesh and lived among human beings. This disclosure gives us an advantage over the characters in the narrative. Their knowledge of Jesus' identity increases as the story unfolds, but we know from the beginning.

Moving through the first three chapters, we encounter at least six designations for Jesus. John the Baptist points out to the crowd that Jesus is "the Lamb of God who takes away the sin of the world" (1:29; cf. 1:36). Andrew tells Simon Peter that he and his friend have found the Messiah (1:41), or, in Philip's words, "him about whom Moses in the law and also the prophets wrote" (1:45). Both John the Baptist and Nathaniel call Jesus "Son of God," and Nathaniel adds yet another title, "the King of Israel" (1:34, 49). These characters function as spokesmen for the author to introduce "Jesus, son of Joseph from Nazareth" (1:45). Jesus is more than a rabbi, even though he is frequently referred to as such (1:38, 49). He is, according to Nicodemus, "a teacher who has come from God" (3:2).

By the time the Samaritan woman encounters Jesus, we already know what she has yet to discover. We find ourselves rooting for her as she first sees Jesus as a thirsty Jewish man, then a prophet, then the Messiah, and eventually the Savior of the world (4:9, 19, 25-26, 29, 42). The parade of titles for Jesus in John 1–3 also lends credibility to Jesus' authority and ability to grant life as the giver of living water in John 4.

The authority of Jesus is another theme that the author has been developing since the beginning of the Gospel. Time and again, the author compares Jesus with the revered institutions of the Judaism of his time ("Second Temple Judaism") and finds him superior. First, Jesus is shown to be superior to the Torah: "The law indeed was given through Moses; grace and truth came through Jesus Christ" (1:17). To illustrate this superiority, the author chooses the changing of water into wine as the first story to reveal Jesus' glory. In this story, Jesus uses the water in six stone jars set aside for purification, turning it into one hundred and twenty gallons of choice wine, the symbol of messianic abundance (2:6-11). This is a powerful statement on Jesus' authority over the law. The life and joy he offers far exceed what the ritual cleansings of the Jewish law can achieve.

Immediately after the miracle at Cana, the author introduces the story of the cleansing of the temple. In this symbolic action, Jesus speaks against the failings of the temple in Jewish political and religious life. Jesus says, "Destroy this temple, and in three days I will raise it up" (2:19). The author then explains that Jesus is referring to his resurrection, identifying his body with the temple (2:21-22). Since the temple signifies the presence of God, Jesus is claiming that he embodies the presence of God. He is the Word "who became flesh and dwelled (the Greek word actually means 'tabernacled') among us" (1:14). In Jesus, the law and the temple/tabernacle—the Jewish institutions of obedience and worship—combine and find their true significance.

The themes of water and temple, introduced in chapter 2, are revisited in Jesus' dialogue with Nicodemus in chapter 3. Here Nicodemus, a Pharisee and leader of the Jews, represents the religious elite among the temple authorities (3:1; cf. 7:45-52). Using the image of new birth, Jesus explains that entry into the kingdom of God requires that one be "born of water and Spirit" (3:5). This echoes God's promise in Ezekiel to cleanse his people with water and put his Spirit in them so that they can follow his statutes (Ezek 36:25-27). Once again, this idea flows naturally into John 4, where Jesus offers the Samaritan woman living water and discusses with her the true place of worship. The creative and life-giving power of the Word, now attributed to Jesus, is further expressed as "a spring of water gushing up to eternal life" (4:14), even more than one hundred and twenty gallons of fine wine.

Now that we have laid historical and theological foundations, we have a better idea of the text's complexity. On the one hand, we follow the time line of Jesus' ministry. We make note of the hostility between Jews and

Samaritans, take into account the many possible underlying factors of the woman's tragic life, and acknowledge the multiple barriers crossed by Jesus to make this encounter a reality. On the other hand, we appreciate the literary artistry of the author, seeing how carefully he builds his case for Jesus' identity. With all this in mind, we are ready to tackle the meaning of worshiping in Spirit and truth.

A Christocentric Reading

The story progresses by means of a series of partial understandings and misunderstandings on the part of the Samaritan woman. First, she is receptive to the idea of living water, but initially thinks of living water as a continuous supply of flowing water (4:11). Next, she rightly sees the importance of worship, but her national history prevents her from thinking of anything else but Mount Gerizim versus Jerusalem (4:20). Finally, she wonders if Jesus is the Messiah, but is still unsure even after Jesus has answered that he is (4:29). Yet each time the woman gains clarity, we move closer to the conclusion that no one is beyond the reach of God's saving mission. In this section, we will consider several elements of this story that focus on Jesus (that is, Christocentric elements): (1) Jesus as the giver of living water; (2) Jesus as the locus of Spirit-empowered worship; and (3) Jesus as both the Messiah of Israel and the Savior of the world.

The humor of the story lies in the woman's surprise at both Jesus' request for literal water and his offer of living water. We can imagine her thinking, "Sir, do you hear what you're saying?" The rift between Jews and Samaritans and the social distance between men and women aside, Jesus does not have a bucket with him. Yet he claims the ability to give her water from a deep well—or at least that is how she understands his offer. Is he going to draw water with his bare hands? Since he claims to provide a continuous supply of water, is he even greater than Jacob, the patriarch of the Samaritans, whose well has never run dry for them all these years? The woman's question is never answered outright, but it goes without saying that Jesus is greater than Jacob, and his water is superior both in efficacy and abundance. It does far more than quench one's thirst for the moment. It is "a spring of water gushing up to eternal life" (4:14), capable of satisfying a person's spiritual thirst forever.

It is difficult to pinpoint what the woman understands and what she misses. When she finally asks Jesus for his living water "so that [she] may never be thirsty or have to keep coming here to draw water" (4:15), is she speaking literally or metaphorically? By not wanting to keep returning to this well to draw water, she appears to be thinking about regular water. Living water—flowing or running water in a stream—is preferable to stagnant water drawn from a well, both in taste and cleanliness. But for her not to want to be thirsty again, is she connecting the image of living water with the promise of eternal life? As the conversation progresses, Jesus' offer seems less absurd to her. She finds the notion of living water more and more attractive. While the woman may not understand perfectly the metaphorical meaning of "living water," the readers are expected to catch the author's drift, thanks to clues already provided in the first three chapters of John and to symbolic referents to water in the Old Testament and other Jewish writings.

Water in the Gospel of John is identified as the Holy Spirit. Later on, at the Feast of Tabernacles, Jesus will say, "Let anyone who is thirsty come to me, and let the one who believes in me drink, as the Scripture has said, 'Out of his heart shall flow rivers of living water'" (7:37-38). With this declaration, Jesus extends his offer to the Samaritan woman to all the pilgrims at the feast. Drawing upon both passages, we conclude that drinking from Jesus means believing in him and, as a result, having eternal life. This eternal life is represented by the image of flowing water in an ever-productive stream. To this invitation the author adds an editorial comment: "Now he said this about the Spirit, which believers in him were to receive" (7:39). The role of the Holy Spirit in bringing about spiritual rebirth is once again highlighted, echoing Jesus' admonition to Nicodemus that he must be born of water and Spirit (3:5; cf. Ezek 36). But who sends the Holy Spirit in John? Just as Jesus provides living water, he also sends the Holy Spirit (15:26; 16:7; 20:22).

In the Old Testament and other Jewish literature, there are ample references to water as a symbol for the Torah. For example, Ben Sira compares the wisdom of the law to the mighty rivers, the Tigris and the Euphrates (Sir 4:25-26). In Proverbs, the fountain of wisdom is described as a gushing stream (Prov 18:4). Identifying the law with water is natural because the Jews believe that following the law will lead to life, and water is essential for sustaining life. The theme of Jesus' superiority resurfaces again, as the Holy Spirit (Jesus' living water) is more effective than the Torah (the Jews' life-giving water) in enabling God's people to live in faithfulness and obedience to God.

Jesus' offer of living water is a call for the woman to receive the Holy Spirit whom he sends. The Holy Spirit cleanses and renews, so that she may be delivered from her "deadly" predicament to the promise and assurance of eternal life. But the conversation cannot end here. The regeneration of this one Samaritan woman will have a rippling effect on her entire community. Not only will the villagers be saved, but their idea of what it means to worship God will undergo a complete upheaval.

The issue of the woman's five husbands moves from the gift of living water to what proper worship entails. The logic is straightforward if we avoid trying to analyze the woman's behavior. Jesus' supernatural knowledge of her past convinces her of his prophetic status. Prophets in the Old Testament made judgments on matters regarding the temple, such as the state of the people's worship and the integrity of the priesthood (Jer 7:1-34; Isa 66:1-4; Mal 1:1-14). Worship is a burning issue for the Samaritans, given that the historical conflicts between the Jews and the Samaritans frequently revolved around their temples. The tone of the woman's query seems matter of fact: "Our ancestors worshiped on this mountain, but you (plural; you [Jews]) say that the place where people must worship is in Jerusalem" (4:21). Since a Jewish prophet is standing in front of her, why not let him rule between the competing claims once and for all?

By way of living water, five husbands, and Jesus as prophet, we finally arrive at the issue of true worship. If we maintain John's identification of living water as the Holy Spirit, then the uncertainty in the translation of 4:23 from Greek to English is at least partly resolved: "But the hour is coming, and is now here, when the true worshipers will worship the Father in Spirit (*pneuma*) and truth." In context, *pneuma* refers to the Holy Spirit, not the spirit of the worshiper.

What, then, is the relationship between Spirit and truth? What does "worship in Spirit and truth" look like? The use of only one preposition, as opposed to two ("*in* Spirit and *in* truth"), allows for a more unified understanding of worship. In other words, "Spirit" and "truth" refer to one reality, not two. Later in the Farewell Discourses, Jesus calls the Holy Spirit "the Spirit of truth" three times (14:17; 15:26; 16:13). When we read *pneuma* as "Spirit" in reference to the divine Spirit, verse 24 follows naturally: "God is Spirit, and those who worship him must worship in Spirit and truth." The Holy Spirit, which is in fact God's Spirit, is the driving force behind all believers' worship.

All this is to say that true worship of God is by definition Spirit-empowered worship. For believers, there is no such thing as worship that is *not* in Spirit and truth, for all believers have the Holy Spirit in them. As Jesus tells the Samaritan woman, true worship is not determined by physical location, whether Jerusalem or Mount Gerizim. Instead, it is centered on him, the embodiment of the temple (2:19-22) and the place of God's presence. Jesus is both the object of worship and the enabler of true worship through his gift of the Holy Spirit. By saying "the hour is coming, and *now is*" (4:23), Jesus takes the perfect worship on the day of future salvation and declares it a present reality. This is possible for believers because he is in their midst.

Jesus' reframing of worship must have made sense to the Samaritan woman, whose next question indicates her understanding that Jesus has moved the discussion onto a different plane. She wonders about the expected Messiah, the one "who will proclaim all things to [them]" (4:25). Since the Samaritans only recognized the five books of Moses, the messianic figure to whom this woman refers is not the royal Davidic king but a teacher-prophet like Moses (Deut 18:18). Whether a Davidic king or a prophet like Moses, she has in mind an agent from God who will teach and guide his people. In reply, Jesus makes one of the few direct claims in all four Gospels of his messianic status: "I am he, the one who is speaking to you" (4:26). Jesus reveals his identity neither to friend nor foe but to the least of the least—a Samaritan woman, a loner not accepted by her own people.

Overwhelmed and excited, the woman abandons her water jar and rushes back to the center of town proclaiming that she may have met the Messiah. One would expect people to dismiss her testimony given her lack of standing in the community. Why do the townspeople believe her? Maybe their curiosity gets the better of them. The text does not say, except that they respond to her invitation, "Come and see" (4:29), just like the first few disciples of Jesus did (1:39, 46). The woman becomes a missionary to her own people, who in turn become believers through her testimony and their later encounter with Jesus (4:39-42).

The story ends with the Samaritans hailing Jesus as "Savior of the world" (4:42), adding to the list of titles given by John the Baptist, Andrew, Philip, Nathaniel, and Nicodemus. By crossing socio-ethnic boundaries to start his conversation with the Samaritan woman, Jesus brings together his Jewish disciples and these new Samaritan believers. He demonstrates that while salvation necessarily begins with the Jews, God's plan of redemption is for the world.

Conclusion

Far too often, the Samaritan woman at the well is portrayed as someone who is suspicious and defensive, whose sinful past is brought into the light because she badly needs cleansing with the living water Jesus provides. Now we have considered the historical and literary elements crucial to her story, and we are challenged to rethink our biases. Regardless of her social status and the fact that Jesus is a prophet, the woman talks to him about spiritually important matters. She may not always capture Jesus' point fully, but she is always heading in the right direction. Over the course of the conversation, she is increasingly able to understand what Jesus offers her—the gift of the Holy Spirit, eternal life, and the means of true worship.

By placing the stories of Nicodemus and the Samaritan woman side by side in chapters 3 and 4, the author intends for us to see a contrast. Nicodemus, the highly regarded leader of the Jews, remains somewhat befuddled at the end of his conversation with Jesus. He comes by night and remains in spiritual darkness. On the contrary, the despised Samaritan woman comes to draw water in broad daylight, a sign of her shame, and yet she emerges from her encounter with Jesus basking in spiritual light and insight.

The significance of this story extends beyond Jesus' compassion for a social outcast. When we read the story with Jesus as our focus, it pulls together themes already introduced in John 1–3 and brings the presentation of Jesus' identity and mission to a mini-climax of sorts, culminating in the Samaritans' embrace of Jesus as Savior of the world. As the giver of living water, Jesus gives eternal life through the Holy Spirit, who in turn enables believers to worship God. True worship no longer depends on location or even a physical temple. Rather, it depends entirely on the person of Jesus, the spiritual temple and embodiment of God's presence.

Seen in this light, the prayer we hear at church, that we "worship God in Spirit and truth," has little to do with our spiritual preparedness and everything to do with God's work through Jesus and the Holy Spirit. We do not empower ourselves; we are empowered to worship in ways beyond our best capabilities. So rather than fretting over our lack of spirituality as we walk into church next time, let us be grateful that even our ability to worship is in and of itself an act of divine grace.

Discussion Questions

1. Before reading this chapter, what did the story of Jesus' encounter with the Samaritan woman mean to you? What did you think of the phrase "worshiping in spirit and in truth"?

2. Compare the way Jesus interacts with the Samaritan woman in John 4 with the way he deals with Nicodemus in John 3. Do you identify more strongly with one character or the other? What can you learn from Jesus' approach to these very different individuals?

3. In this chapter, I interpret John 4 as saying that the Holy Spirit aids our worship of God. If this is true, how do we actively participate in worship? How do we avoid merely going through the motions and "letting God do all the work"?

4. In this story, the gospel of salvation is shared through an unexpected channel—a village outcast whom people would rather avoid or ignore. Have you ever known someone who surprised you or others by conveying an important message from God?

For Further Reading

Dale C. Allison Jr., "The Living Water," *St. Vladimir's Theological Quarterly* 30 (1986): 143–57.

George R. Beasley-Murray, *John*, 2nd ed. (Word Biblical Commentary 36; Waco: Word, 1999).

Jo Ann Davidson, "John 4: Another Look at the Samaritan Woman," *Andrews University Seminary Studies* 43 (2005): 159–68.

Craig S. Keener, *The Gospel of John: A Commentary*, vol. 1 (Peabody: Hendrickson, 2003).

Craig R. Koester, *Symbolism in the Fourth Gospel: Meaning, Mystery, Community*, 2nd ed. (Minneapolis: Fortress, 2003).

Jerome H. Neyrey, "What's Wrong with this Picture? John 4, Cultural Stereotypes of Women, and Public and Private Space," *Biblical Theology Bulletin* 24 (1994): 77–91.

Chapter 3

The Vine and Its Branches

John 15:5

Growing up in a densely populated city like Hong Kong where most people live in tightly packed apartments with no garden or courtyard space, I never developed a green thumb. I can hardly name trees, let alone know what to do with flowers and shrubs. Now that I live in an American suburb, I enjoy looking at the greenery around me, even though I have no idea what to do with the plants in my yard.

On both sides of my front door are four white hydrangea bushes, planted five years ago. Since then, without any intervention on my part, they have grown taller, leafier, and more abundant in blooms. Every year, they produce hardy white flowers that withstand the worst thunderstorms in my area.

It is hard to manage their rapid growth. Last summer, there were so many hydrangea blooms that their weight sent the stalks bending toward the ground. Other branches grew sideways in search of open areas and light, invading the space of nearby plants. This resulted in the blooms sitting like snowballs on top of the mulch. I was getting too much of a good thing. In an act of desperation, I took the garden shears and cut down as much of the greenery as I could. I assumed that my "pruning," which left each hydrangea to face the winter snow looking like a clump of short wooden spikes, would stunt some growth the following spring and keep the plants under control.

This spring, ironically, the hydrangeas returned with a vengeance, thanks to plenty of rain and mild temperatures. At the peak of summer, the bushes are now bigger than before, with more leaves and blooms than ever! If this is the result of my random pruning, I cannot imagine what would happen with proper care and tending.

Meanwhile, not far from the hydrangeas sits a Japanese maple tree with a different problem. Overall the tree is healthy, with luscious green leaves that turn a flaming red in the autumn—except for one section. There, I see bare branches and twigs still attached to the tree, but they show no signs of life. This appears to be a dead spot within an otherwise vibrant plant. While hope springs eternal for this amateur gardener that perhaps the branches are dormant but not dead, after about four years, I am ready to give up and cut off the dead wood.

My hydrangea bushes and Japanese maple tree remind me of Jesus' vine and branches discourse in John 15:1-8. Unlike Jesus' audience in ancient Palestine, I live nowhere near a vineyard and am not familiar with the behavior of vines and the process of growing grapes for wine. A brief visit to Napa Valley, California, does not make me an authority on tending vines. Given the effects of my brutal pruning of the hydrangeas, I begin to appreciate what Jesus means when he says the vinedresser prunes fruit-bearing branches in order for them to bear more fruit (15:2). The Japanese maple also suggests that it is possible to have dead branches on an otherwise vibrant plant, similar to those removed and finally discarded by the vinedresser (15:2, 6).

These analogies, of course, are imperfect. We know better than to use hydrangeas and Japanese maples to understand vines, yet we sometimes do the same with biblical interpretation. If I want to understand the image in John 15, I would be better off obtaining some knowledge of vine-growing practices in the ancient world.

It makes sense not to use hydrangeas and Japanese maples to understand vines, yet we sometimes do the opposite with biblical interpretation. Borrowing passages from other New Testament books to explain the one in front of us can result in a misreading of the text. Modern readers tend to do this quite easily. Even though we regard the entire Bible as one work, it is at the same time a collection of works by different authors, written at specific times and places for specific audiences. The ancient audience would not have encountered the range of New Testament writings now available to us. They most likely would not have gone to the letters of Paul or the book of Hebrews to help them understand what they heard from the Gospel of John. However, modern readers who have access to the entire New Testament often impose meaning on Jesus' words about the vine and its branches. If we are not mindful of grounding our approach in the text's historical and literary contexts, we too may allow our experience and preconceived notions to drown out its message.

Boundaries of Interpretation

At first glance, the image in John 15 seems simple: God is the vinedresser, Jesus is the vine, and his disciples are the branches (15:1, 5). The vinedresser prunes the vine either by helping fruit-bearing branches be even more productive or by removing those that have become useless. Complications arise, however, when we try to define fruit-bearing and pruning, or explain what it means to be a dead branch on a live tree, without giving attention to the literary context of the passage.

For example, we might assume that the fruit Jesus wants the branches to bear is the fruit of the Spirit Paul names in his letter to the Galatians: love, joy, peace, patience, kindness, generosity, faithfulness, gentleness, and self-control (Gal 5:22-23). This assumption lacks textual support, for nowhere in the Gospel do we get the impression that John's usage of the metaphor is identical to Paul's. Even so, with a list of these nine qualities that we often fail to exhibit, some Christians may fear that if they fail to bear the fruit of joy or peace, then they become like branches that do not bear fruit and will be cut off by God, the vinedresser. This is a frightening proposition. If this were the case, would anyone be left on the vine?

Since pruning sounds like something painful yet beneficial, we might think it refers to suffering, in light of scriptural passages like these:

> Whenever you face trials of any kind, consider it nothing but joy, because you know that the testing of your faith produces endurance; and let endurance have its full effect, so that you may be mature and complete, lacking in nothing. (Jas 1:2-3)

> In this you rejoice, even if now for a little while you have had to suffer various trials, so that the genuineness of your faith—being more precious than gold that, though perishable, is tested by fire—may be found to result in praise and glory and honor when Jesus Christ is revealed. (1 Pet 1:6-7)

These passages indicate that God uses suffering to nurture faith, so that we may mature in Christ through times of trials. While it is often the case that we do grow spiritually in difficulties, the question is whether this is what the author of John means by pruning.

In order to explain the presence of dead branches on a healthy vine, we might look to the parable of the wheat and the weeds, even though it is found in Matthew but not in John (Matt 13:24-30). The picture of the wheat and weeds existing together in the field parallels that of a vine with live and dead branches on it. In the end, the weeds and the dead branches will both be burned. According to this reading, Jesus' picture of the vine and its varied branches represents the presence of all sorts of Christians in the church today, including "dead branches" who think they are Christians but are not actually saved. Thinking of the text this way leads to speculation of the fate of nominal Christians, "pew-warmers," or whomever else we consider as spiritually under par in the Christian community.

In addition, the possibility of a Christian (a branch on the vine) being burned by the vinedresser might not sit well with those who believe in eternal salvation. Surely a truly regenerated Christian, even a dead branch, could not lose his or her salvation, because this person has to be a Christian in order to be found on the vine in the first place! For the text to fit this doctrine, the phrase "abiding in me" (15:4-7) must refer to the continuing process of being made right, while the phrase "in me" (15:2) refers to one's initial justification in Christ. According to this kind of reasoning, a Christian can still be "in Christ" (that is, "saved") even though he or she may not be "abiding in Christ" or "staying close to Jesus" all the time. While not in an ideal situation, this believer will not lose his or her salvation on account of spiritual immaturity and fruitlessness, only the future reward. This interpretation appeals to Paul's letter to the Corinthians for support: "If the work is burned up, the builder will suffer loss; the builder will be saved, but only as through fire" (1 Cor 3:15). It is worth wondering, however, if some people make the distinction between "in me" and "abide in me" only to make the text support their theological position.

In and of themselves, the ideas that affect our reading of the text in John contain some elements of truth. It is natural for a Spirit-filled Christian to produce the fruit of the Spirit. Suffering is indeed a spiritual training ground, for even Jesus learns obedience through suffering (Heb 5:8). False followers of Jesus will ultimately face God's judgment. Jesus warns in the Sermon on the Mount that lip service to his lordship is insufficient for entry into the kingdom of heaven (Matt 7:21-22). Common among these interpretations, however, is the importing of other passages outside the Gospel of John to explain the text. If using hydrangeas and Japanese maple to explain vines is inappropriate, it is also not right to base our understanding of the Gospel of John on the writings of Paul, Matthew, James, and Peter rather than on John.

Instead, consider the following questions that pay attention to the historical and literary contexts relevant to the text:

1. At what point in Jesus' earthly mission does he use the image of the vine and branches to teach his disciples?

2. Since John 15:1-8 is part of a much longer conversation known as the Farewell Discourses (John 13–17), how do the themes in this passage fit into the rest of Jesus' parting words to his disciples?

3. How does knowledge of growing grapevines and making wine (that is, viticulture) in the ancient Mediterranean world help our understanding of the image of the vine and its branches?

4. What additional symbolism does the image of the vine carry that would be immediately apparent to Jesus' Jewish disciples?

As we will see, the vine and branches passage is Jesus' word of encouragement to his disciples on the eve of his death. The discourse focuses mainly on the disciples' need to maintain their dependence on Jesus. This is especially crucial when, under the circumstances, giving up the faith is a real temptation and persecution a real threat. Just as the survival of the branches depends on the vine, so the disciples can draw life from none other than Jesus. As they experience his love for them, they in turn will be able to love one another and bear the fruit that gives evidence of the life in them.

The Farewell Discourses of John 13–17

Chapters 13 to 17 of the Gospel of John contain elements one would find in the parting speech a respected person gives his or her family and community as death draws near. Examples of this genre are found in the farewell discourses of Jacob (Gen 48–49), Moses (Deut 31–34), Joshua (Josh 23–24), and David (2 Chr 28–29). Typically, the dying person reviews his or her life and projects into the future. Past achievements are recounted and a successor is named. Warnings are sounded and instructions given to those who remain. The speech then closes with blessings and prayers.

All these elements are present in Jesus' Farewell Discourses. He refers to his approaching death as the hour in which he will leave the world and return to his Father (12:23, 27; 13:1; 16:32; 17:1). Reviewing his life, Jesus claims that he has accomplished everything the Father sent him to do. He has revealed the Father to those who believe in him and shown them the way to eternal life (14:6-11; 15:15; 17:1-8). To continue his work after his departure, Jesus promises to send the Spirit of Truth. The Holy Spirit is Jesus' "successor" who will remind the disciples of his teachings (14:16-17, 26; 15:26; 16:7-14). Jesus then extends an invitation to his disciples to enter into union with him and his Father. To do so, he commands them to remain in his love and to love one another (14:21-23; 15:1-17). The discourse closes with Jesus praying for the protection of and unity among his disciples as well as for those who will believe in him through their witness (17:1-26).

A careful reader might notice two oddities within these chapters. First is an awkward transition at the end of John 14, where Jesus says, "Rise, let us be on our way" (14:31). This verse would have flowed naturally into chapter 18: "After Jesus had spoken these words, he went out with his disciples across the Kidron Valley to a place where there was a garden" (18:1). Instead, the vine and branches discourse in chapter 15 sets off another sequence of conversation and prayer that lasts until the end of chapter 17. The second oddity is Jesus' comment that none of the disciples asks him where he is going when he announces his departure (16:5). This contradicts the exact question Thomas has posed earlier asking Jesus about his destination (14:5). These inconsistencies suggest that John 15–17 might have been an insertion into an earlier draft that went directly from 14:31 to 18:1.

Despite these minor glitches, the version we now have displays a strong literary unity across all five chapters. The themes in chapters 13–14 are often repeated and developed in 15–17, so that the entire discourse reads as an integrated whole. In particular, reading 13:1-30 and 15:1-10 alongside each other is instructive. Peter and Judas in chapter 13 function as examples of the two types of branches in chapter 15. Through challenging circumstances, Peter proves himself to be a branch that ultimately remains on the vine, whereas Judas cuts himself off from his source of life and ends up a withered branch destined for destruction.

Peter and Judas in John 13

The opening verse of chapter 13 not only introduces the Farewell Discourses but also introduces the entire Passion Narrative by announcing the timing and significance of Jesus' death: "Now before the festival of the Passover, Jesus knew that his hour had come to depart from the world and go to the Father. Having loved his own who were in the world, he loved them to the end" (13:1).

For the Jews, the festival of the Passover heightens the expectation of God to bring about his promised deliverance of Israel. The God who saved Israel from the hands of the Egyptians will again save his people from their enemies, this time the Romans. Jesus' disciples would hardly have imagined that this second exodus would come by way of the Messiah's death. Up to this point, Jesus' enemies could not harm him because "his hour had not yet come" (7:30; 8:20). But now the ominous note, "his hour had come," signifies that the narrative is moving toward the climax of Jesus' mission (12:27; cf. 12:32-33). As the author puts it, Jesus loves his disciples "to the end (*telos*)"—to the utmost degree and to the end of his life. It is fitting that the last words of Jesus on the cross in this Gospel are "It is finished (*tetelestai*)" (19:30). Sharing the same root word in the Greek, *telos* and *tetelestai* both signify a sense of finality and accomplishment. Like bookends at the beginning and end of the Passion Narrative, they remind the readers that Jesus' love is epitomized by his death.

Seen in this light, the foot-washing event takes on a meaning beyond humility, which alone does not fully explain Jesus' answer to Peter's objection. Given the dusty roads of ancient villages, the custom of having one's feet washed before reclining at a meal was both practical and ceremonial. Foot-washing was a menial task left to the lowliest of servants. Peter's embarrassment is expected. Jesus, his host and teacher, breaks social norms by taking on the role of a servant and washing his disciples' feet. Horrified, Peter issues a protest in the strongest of terms: "No! No! No! Never in a million years will you ever wash my feet!" (13:8).

If Jesus' intention was simply to show his disciples what it meant to be a humble servant (13:14), his answer to Peter, "Unless I wash you, you have no share with me" (13:8), would seem enigmatic. But if heard against the backdrop of Jesus' self-giving death and love for Peter, then Jesus' words are as heart-wrenching as Peter's protest. First, Jesus says, "Unless *I* wash *you* . . . ." Peter cannot wash himself; he must be on the receiving end of Jesus' washing. While a Jew can self-administer ritualistic cleansing, the purification Jesus is talking about can only be performed by Jesus through his upcoming death. Second, Peter's refusal of what Jesus is about to do will cause him to lose his inheritance in Jesus. Rejecting Jesus' washing will lead to Peter's rejection from the family of God's people.

The stakes are high. Jesus' action, however unexpected to Peter and his fellow disciples, symbolizes and foreshadows his self-giving death on their behalf. What Jesus will soon accomplish on the cross will far surpass the humbling of a respected leader as he washes the feet of his followers. Peter's salvation is a gift for which he can take no credit. Receiving this gesture of love anticipates an eternal fellowship that Peter will have with Jesus.

The full meaning of Jesus' action will be appreciated later. All that Jesus requires of Peter now is obedience and receptivity (13:7). It is unclear how much Peter grasps the significance of Jesus' words, for he overcompensates and asks for his head and hands to be cleaned as well. Even so, his eagerness shows that he is on the right track. Jesus reassures him that washing his feet alone will cover the spiritual cleansing of his entire person (13:9-10).

By contrast, Judas repeatedly rejects Jesus' gift of grace. Since Jesus washes the feet of all twelve disciples, Judas has the same opportunity as Peter to respond to Jesus' cleansing. Even though the text does not record Judas's reaction to the foot-washing, it is implied in Jesus' comment to Peter, "And you are clean, *though not all of you*" (13:10). To make sure readers catch this detail, the author adds, "For [Jesus] knew who was to betray him; for this reason he said, 'Not all of you are clean'" (13:11).

After the foot-washing event, Jesus reveals to his disciples that one of them will betray him. He even identifies his betrayer as the one to whom he will give a piece of bread, and then proceeds to dip some in the dish and hand it to Judas (13:21-27). When a host gives his guest a piece of bread in this manner, it is a sign of hospitality. Whatever confusion exists among the disciples, Judas seems to know that Jesus refers to him. Jesus invites Judas to reverse course. The author notes the irony of the situation, matching a double reference to Satan entering into Judas with another double reference to Judas taking the bread from Jesus (13:1, 27, 30). With his gesture of love and hospitality rejected twice, Jesus finally tells Judas to go and do quickly what he is about to do (13:27). Judas has crossed from the presence of the light of the world into the sinister darkness of evil. The author pointedly closes this segment: "And it was night" (13:30).

The stories of Peter and Judas are helpful boundaries for our interpretation of the image of the vine and branches in chapter 15. If we bear in mind the Farewell Discourses and especially these two characters, we are less likely to impose materials outside of the Gospel of John onto the text. Given the circumstances under which Jesus delivers these words, the immediate focus is not on the daily struggles of Christians to be joyful, peaceful, patient, kind, and so forth, as in Paul's list of the fruit of the Spirit. These qualities are not unimportant, but the issue here is a choice between commitment and apostasy in the face of persecution. The fruit in view must be related to what it takes to stay connected to or abide in Jesus. The natural image is especially fitting for describing such a relationship because without the vine, the branches will eventually die.

I Am the True Vine: Jesus as Mediator

Among the four Gospels, unique to John are seven "I am" statements of Jesus:

- "I am the bread of life" (6:35, 48).
- "I am the light of the world" (8:12; 9:5).
- "I am the gate" (10:7, 9).
- "I am the good shepherd" (10:11, 14).
- "I am the resurrection and the life" (11:25).
- "I am the way, the truth, and the life" (14:6).
- "I am the true vine" (15:1; cf. 15:5).

Each of these statements has to do with Jesus' life-giving and life-preserving power. The last statement, "I am the true vine," is distinctive as it points in two directions. On the one hand, Jesus makes the claim of his divine identity with the use of "I am." On the other hand, he affirms his heritage as a superior Israelite by identifying himself as "the true vine."

The words "I am" (*egō eimi* in the Greek) on the lips of Jesus allude to the revered name of God in the Old Testament. According to the Septuagint, the Greek translation of the Hebrew Scriptures, God answers Moses when asked for his name, "I am the one who is (*egō eimi ho ōn*)" (Exod 3:14). Elsewhere in Isaiah, the double use of this self-designation underscores the fact that no one else but God is the Savior of Israel. For example, God says, "I, even I, am He (*egō eimi, egō eimi*) who blots out your transgressions" (Isa 43:25; see also 48:12; 51:12). In the Gospel of John, Jesus, the Son of God and Word made flesh, is the mediator of God's salvation. Authorized by God to give life, Jesus represents and reveals the Father perfectly by doing exactly what the Father tells him to say and do, so that seeing him is the same as seeing the Father (5:19-24, 26-27, 30, 36-38). In this way, each "I am" statement of Jesus is an expression of his divine identity. He acts on behalf of God for the benefit of God's people.

Jesus the divine Son and agent is at the same time the Messiah, the King of Israel who stands in solidarity with God's people (1:49). When Jesus refers to himself as the true vine, the allusion to Israel as God's vine or vineyard—a common image in the Psalms and the Prophets—is inescapable. Planted by God as a choice vine, Israel yielded wild grapes and became useless. In the end the vineyard owner let it run wild or had it burned (Ps 80:8-15; Isa 5:1-6; Jer 2:21; Ezek 15:1-8; 19:10-14). The vine illustrates Israel's tragic historical patterns of unfaithfulness and rebellion against God, resulting in judgment and exile. By contrast, as the *true* vine, Jesus now embodies what it means to be God's people in every sense of the word. He loves the Father with his faithfulness, obedience, and total dependence. He is the vine that responds positively to the vinedresser's pruning.

The statement, "I am the true vine," represents Jesus as the life-giving link between God and God's people. On the one hand, he mediates the love and life of God to those he gathers around himself. He is the vine that supports the branches and keeps them alive. On the other hand, the vine is pleasing to the vinedresser only when all its branches are healthy and bearing fruit.

Viticulture in the Ancient Mediterranean

It is unlikely that Jesus expects all his disciples to be expert vinedressers in order to understand the metaphor. Vineyards were abundant in ancient Palestine and around the Mediterranean, so most people would have had some understanding of the annual cycle of tending vines.

Specific practices may vary depending on climate, soil condition, and terrain, but the yearly cycle moves from spring planting to summer harvest, fall pruning, and winter dormancy. Details of planting, the training of branches, and harvesting are not necessary for our purposes; we are interested in the types of pruning given to a vine at different times. The goal of the vinedresser is to maximize yield and maintain a healthy vine for the following year. To do so, a balance needs to be struck between the amount and quality of the grapes and the speed and spread of the growth.

In the spring, prior to blooming, some shoots are pinched off to direct energy to the remaining ones with fruit-bearing potential. Too many growth points spread the nutrients too thin and result in small clusters that grow too slowly. Extra foliage that drains energy is cut away, though not all leafy non-fruiting branches are removed. Since branches that do not bear fruit one season may do so the next, planning ahead is important when selecting which branch or shoot to trim. After the harvest, the whole vine undergoes heavy pruning. All remaining leaves and dead branches are removed and burned. The vine then survives the winter months with little expense of energy until the spring when the cycle starts again. The entire process is labor intensive and delicate, as each branch is treated individually according to its strength and potential. Only an experienced vinedresser knows when and where to apply the pruning knife.

This brief explanation of pruning allows us to appreciate its two purposes—(1) to enhance the productivity of branches that are already fruitful and (2) to limit the waste of energy on branches that do not bear fruit. In John 15, Jesus describes only two types of branches: productive, fruiting branches and dead, non-fruiting branches. Nothing is said of leafy but non-fruiting branches that are still alive. Although such foliage does exist on a vine in a real vineyard, there's no need for Jesus to include all types of branches in his metaphor. His simplified picture highlights the contrast between the best and the worst types of branches without the distraction of "in-between" categories. Useful branches are pruned and useless branches are destroyed.

Pruning and Cleansing

Lost in our English translation, the Greek play on words in the following verses provides clues to help us uncover the meaning of pruning:

- "He removes (*airei*) every branch in me that bears no fruit." (15:2a)
- "Every branch that bears fruit he prunes (*kathairei*) to make it bear more fruit." (15:2b)
- "You have already been cleansed (*katharoi*) by the word that I have spoken to you." (15:3)

Airei ("he removes"), *kathairei* ("he prunes"), and *katharoi* ("cleansed") comprise two overlapping sets of puns. The first set is *airei* and *kathairei*. These two words set up a contrast between the removal (*airei*) of branches that do not bear fruit and the pruning (*kathairei*) of those that do. Technically, removing a fruitless branch is also part of the larger pruning process, but for the sake of clarity the author uses the verb "prune" only for the fruitful branches. It is expected that the vinedresser will return time and again to prune the fruitful branches as long as they remain productive. Pruning requires the vinedresser's ongoing tending of the vine. As for the fruitless ones, they are removed, then "gathered, thrown into the fire, and burned" (15:6). This is a one-time event. Once removed, the burned branch cannot be reattached; its connection with the vine and the vinedresser is forever severed.

The second word play occurs between *kathairei* and *katharoi*. Both words come from the same root word, implying that the ideas of pruning and cleansing are mutually interpretive. However, moving from verse 2 to verse 3, Jesus steps out of the metaphor. First he speaks of the plant, "Every

branch that bears fruit he prunes (*kathairei*) . . . ," then he directs a comment
to his disciples: "*You* have already been cleansed (*katharoi*) by the word that
I have spoken to you." Although pruning can be thought of as a form of
cleansing the vine, the reference to the disciples who have already been
cleansed casts a backward glance at the foot-washing episode of chapter 13
where Jesus declares Peter *clean* (*katharos*, 13:8, 10). Now the disciples, Peter
included, are already *cleansed* by Jesus' word (15:3).

The clues left by the puns *kathairei* ("he prunes") and *katharoi*
("cleansed") suggest that whatever meaning we apply to one metaphor must
make sense in the context of the other. Interpreting pruning as suffering and
trials is awkward because it does not work with the idea of "being cleansed
by Jesus' word." Sure, God allows Christians to endure difficult times to reap
the fruit of deepened faith, but this is not what John 15:3 is referring to. A
better strategy is to let the meaning arise from the text itself. The verb for
pruning appears only once in the Gospel of John, so we do not have other
verses in John to explore its usage. However, because it is matched with the
notion of cleansing through the Greek play on words, we can start with
katharoi ("cleansed") and work our way back to *kathairei* ("he prunes").
When the faithful branches are pruned, they are cleansed by Jesus' word.

Those who are "cleansed by Jesus' word" (15:3) have Jesus' words abiding in them (15:7). What "word" of Jesus is in view here? Throughout the
Gospel of John, Jesus the incarnate Word takes the word of truth from the
Father and gives it to his disciples (3:34; 14:24; 17:8, 14, 17). In response,
the disciples are shown to believe in Jesus' word (2:22; 4:50), keep his word
(8:51; 14:23), and continue in his word (8:31). The "word" that cleanses the
disciples is not a single word or speech, but includes all the messages of eternal life that Jesus has related to them all along (6:63, 68). As they believe
what Jesus says of himself, receive him as the one sent from God to effect
their salvation, dwell in his love for them, and commit themselves to obey
his commandments, they are made clean and invited into a lasting relationship with the Father, Son, and Spirit.

This relationship is nurtured by the vinedresser's continuous tending of
the vine. He prunes the branches so that they will be even more productive
than they already are. The next question, then, is what it means to bear fruit
in the context of this image and that of the Farewell Discourses in general.

Bearing the Fruit of Love

Fruit-bearing is a major theme in the vine and branches discourse, appearing
six times in the span of seven verses (15:2, 4, 5, 8). To stay alive and bear

fruit, a branch must be attached to the vine. To bear more fruit, it must be pruned by the vinedresser. The abundant and high-quality fruit is evidence of a branch that is completely dependent on the vine, its source of water, nutrients, and life. Only then can it do what it is supposed to do, which is to bear fruit. Separated from the vine, not only will a branch be unable to bear fruit, but it will die.

Despite his frequent mentioning of fruit-bearing, Jesus does not point out exactly what he means by it. Rather than bringing in other texts (e.g., Gal 5:22), we are best served by staying within the Farewell Discourses. As we shall see, fruit-bearing in the immediate context refers to the disciples' love for one another, which is a direct result of their remaining in Jesus' love.

Drawing from John 15, we note five characteristics of fruit-bearing:

1. It is a repeatable action. A healthy branch does not bear fruit only once. It is pruned in order to improve the quantity and quality of the yield: "Each branch that bears fruit he prunes to make it bear more fruit" (15:2).

2. It depends on divine help. The driving force for ongoing life and growth of a fruiting branch comes not from itself but from the vine to which it is attached: "Just as the branch cannot bear fruit by itself unless it abides in the vine, neither can you unless you abide in me. . . . those who abide in me and I in them bear much fruit, because apart from me you can do nothing" (15:4-5).

3. It is a means of glorifying God. When the whole vine is fruitful, it brings pleasure and praise to the vinedresser: "My Father is glorified by this, that you bear much fruit and become my disciples" (15:8).

4. It is a commandment of Jesus: "I appointed you to go and bear fruit" (15:16a).

5. It will have a far-reaching effect. It is a "fruit that will last" (15:16b).

An obvious place to begin is the fourth characteristic, that fruit-bearing is a commandment of Jesus. In the Farewell Discourses, Jesus indeed issues a specific command to his disciples: "I give you a new commandment, that you love one another" (13:34); "This is my commandment, that you love one another as I have loved you" (15:12); "I am giving you these commands so that you may love one another" (15:17). Assuming for the moment that "loving one another" is what fruit-bearing is all about, we need to test our interpretation against the other four characteristics of fruit-bearing.

To begin with, love yields love (characteristic #1). The more the disciples love one another, the more they are able to continue to do so as a virtuous cycle is set in motion. Loving one another, however, requires divine help (#2). The only way the branches can thrive is to receive nourishment from the vine. The disciples' source of love is Jesus, who loves them in the same way the Father has loved him (15:9). If the disciples are to bear the fruit of love, the love they give to one another must be empowered by and modeled after divine love. In addition, love among the disciples glorifies the Father because a loving community is a witness in a hostile environment (#3 and #5). If there is love among the disciples, their unity will become visible to outsiders. By their love for one another, the Father is revealed to the world, who in response will acknowledge that they are indeed Jesus' disciples (13:35).

Since a healthy vine is recognized by its fruit, it makes sense that fruit-bearing refers to the disciples' love for one another. The vinedresser plants the vine, the vine gives rise to branches, and the branches produce fruit. By the same token, love flows from the Father to the Son, then from the Son to the disciples. To love one another, the disciples must abide in Jesus, just as a branch must abide in the vine in order to bear fruit (15:4).

Abiding as Mutual Indwelling

Intertwined with the images of a vinedresser pruning the vine and the vine empowering healthy branches to bear fruit is the theme of abiding. The Greek verb *menō* may be translated "abide," "remain," or "stay." Occurring eleven times in this passage, it confronts Jesus' disciples and the readers of the Gospel with the fact that this abiding relationship benefits both parties and needs to be maintained (15:4, 5, 6, 7, 9, 10).

As with all mutually beneficial relationships, the disciples' abiding in Jesus is reciprocated in kind by Jesus:

- "Abide in me as I abide in you." (15:4)
- "Those who abide in me and I in them bear much fruit, because apart from me you can do nothing." (15:5)
- "If you abide in me, and my words abide in you, ask for whatever you wish, and it will be done for you." (15:9)

While there are minor variations in the phrasing, such as "abide in my love" (15:10) instead of "abide in me" (15:4), or "my words abide in you" (15:9) as opposed to "I abide in you" (15:4), the essential idea is the same. A union exists between Jesus and his disciples. The image of a vine and its branches is fitting for illustrating this flow of life and love between Jesus and his disciples because it is dynamic, organic, and continuous.

The concept of "abiding in" or "remaining in" one another implies "mutual indwelling," an idea already introduced in John 14. The union between Jesus and his disciples is grounded in the union that already exists between Jesus and his Father. Using phrasing similar to that in chapter 15, Jesus twice declares, "I am in the Father and the Father is in me" (14:10, 11). When the two pairs of relationships are put together—one between the Father and the Son, the other between the Son and his disciples—the resulting circle of mutuality is enlarged. If the disciples abide in Jesus, not only will Jesus abide in them, but the Father will as well.

When Jesus tells his disciples that he is going away in order to prepare a place for them in his Father's house, he assures them that he will return for them so that the disciples may forever be in the presence of Jesus and his Father (14:1-4). On the one hand, the disciples are brought into the dwelling of God. On the other hand, Jesus promises the disciples that the Father and the Son will dwell in them as well: "Those who love me will keep my word, and my Father will love them, and we will come to them and make our home with them" (14:23). Through Jesus, the disciples will enjoy eternal union with God as members of the Father's household. Seen in this light, the imperative to abide in Jesus is above all an invitation of grace.

Peter and Judas: Fruitful and Fruitless Branches

The image of Jesus as the true vine and his disciples as its branches is powerful. Its organic nature is fitting for depicting dynamic relationships. Connected to the vine, a branch thrives and produces fruit that is evidence of the life within. To the contrary, without the vine a branch is dead. It will be cut off and discarded. The possibility of a branch being severed from the vine is what is at stake when Jesus addresses his disciples shortly before his arrest and crucifixion. Commitment or apostasy—these are the choices for the disciples in the upper room as Jesus bids them farewell. If the world hates Jesus, they will hate his disciples too (15:18-20; 17:14-16). Under the threat of persecution, the temptation to fall away from faith looms large. Unless they totally depend on Jesus' love and words, and abide in them, the disciples will not remain united. But as they abide in Jesus' love and show love for one another, the protection of the Father and the presence of the Spirit will sustain them in Jesus' absence.

Throughout the Gospel of John, we see in Peter a branch clinging stubbornly onto the vine. When other followers desert Jesus, Peter refuses to leave, for to him the words of Jesus are "the words of eternal life" (6:68). Despite his initial resistance to letting Jesus wash his feet, Peter accepts his master's overture of love, both as a prelude to Jesus' ultimate act of love on the cross and as a promise of a share in Jesus' inheritance (13:8-9). After denying Jesus three times (18:15-18, 25-27), Peter still returns to Jesus over and over again. He is among the first to run to the tomb after learning from Mary Magdalene that the stone has been rolled away (20:3). He jumps out of the boat and wades toward Jesus as soon as he recognizes him (21:7). He declares his love for Jesus three times, reversing each of his prior denials (21:15-17). Because Jesus has laid down his life for him and welcomed him back, Peter is now able to take on the task of leading the church, even though following Jesus will cost him his life (21:18-19). Indeed, Peter is a branch that has been pruned in order to become more fruitful. His denials do not brand him an apostate because he comes back and is once again made clean.

By contrast, Judas represents a branch that no longer deserves to be on the vine. Not only has Judas rejected Jesus, but he also has rejected his fellow disciples. He does not have love for Jesus or for his community. Even though he allows Jesus to wash his feet, he does not embrace the meaning of Jesus' action. Even though he eats the bread Jesus gives him, he repays Jesus' act of hospitality with an act of betrayal (13:21-30; 18:1-5). Judas never turns back; his apostasy seals his own fate.

In a way, Judas represents a branch that has already died while still hanging on the vine. Nowhere in the discourse, however, does Jesus address how a branch attached to the vine can dry up on its own. Aside from the author's two comments about Satan's role in Judas's decision to betray Jesus (13:2, 27), much is left unexplained. But one thing is sure: at some point—though exactly when or why we do not know—Judas stops drawing on the life of the vine. This branch is no longer capable of bearing fruit and has to be removed by the vinedresser. It has become a piece of dead wood, useless except for burning.

Conclusion

Within the context of John 13–17, the message in the image of the vine and its branches is not difficult to grasp. The more the disciples feel pressured to separate from Jesus, the more he tells them to remain in his love. Without Jesus, his followers can do nothing. In fact, without Jesus, we, too, will experience spiritual and eternal death.

This text is not about the struggles of one's individual daily Christian walk, whether temptation, trial, or the inability to bear "the fruit of the Spirit." It is even less a text about a condemning vinedresser who cannot wait to rid his vine of any branch that commits the slightest infraction. Jesus focuses much more on the life and fruitfulness of the abiding branches than on the loss of the dead ones. At the eve of his death, what his disciples need most is encouragement to persevere, not the threat of destruction.

Looking at the big picture, Jesus' metaphor addresses a decision of life and death. If we choose life and commitment to Jesus, we do so in the context of our place among the community of believers. Jesus presents us with a corporate image, as a solitary branch does not make a vine. As one among many called to be Jesus' disciples, each of us is a member of Israel gathered around Jesus the true vine. Collectively, we are linked not only to our immediate communities of faith, but to all God's people across time and space. This text should broaden our mindset and encourage us to think positively about love and collaboration among communities of faith. If the worldwide church, drawing its life from Jesus, the vine, comes together in unity, it will bring glory to God through the fruit of its effective global witness.

Discussion Questions

1. What does "abiding in Christ" look like? What kinds of pictures come to your mind when you think of it? What experience or practices help illustrate what it means for you to abide in Christ and have Christ abide in you? Is it possible to explain this abiding to someone who is not a believer?

2. In what way does the metaphor of the vine and its branches support, qualify, or challenge the idea that "once saved, we are always saved"?

3. Jesus warns his disciples that apart from him they can do nothing. In a culture of self-sufficiency, how would you walk the fine line between

participating in the work of God's kingdom and maintaining dependence on God for direction and insight? What causes you to slide from depending on God to depending on your own resources and capabilities?

4. In John 15, Jesus tells his disciples to bear the fruit of love for one another. This command is both straightforward and difficult to follow, even among Christians. With your own Christian community in mind, can you identify areas where you stumble and come up with creative solutions?

For Further Reading

George R. Beasley-Murray, *John*, 2nd ed. (Word Biblical Commentary 36; Waco: Word, 1999).

George Johnston, "The Allegory of the Vine: An Exposition of John 15:1-17," *Canadian Journal of Theology* 3 (1957): 150–58.

Craig S. Keener, *The Gospel of John: A Commentary*, vol. 2 (Peabody: Hendrickson, 2003).

Craig R. Koester, *Symbolism in the Fourth Gospel: Meaning, Mystery, Community*, 2nd ed. (Minneapolis: Fortress, 2003).

Chapter 4

The Conflicted Person and All Things Work Together for Good

Romans 7:14-25; 8:28

At first glance, it may seem unusual to look at Romans 7:14-25 and 8:28 in a single discussion. Normally the two do not come as a pair. Romans 7:14-25 describes a conflicted person who cannot do what he wants to do and does the very thing he hates. Romans 8:28 is an all-time favorite: "We know that God makes all things work together for good for those who love God, who are called according to his purpose." Typically these passages are cited in unrelated settings, whether a sermon, a Bible study, or conversations among Christians. Some may identify with the conflicted person of Romans 7:14-25, who sounds like one struggling to shed addictive behavior while striving to do God's will. To the cry of despair, "Wretched man (or woman) that I am," readers may respond, "So am I!" Others may quote Romans 8:28 as a prayer or word of encouragement when deep despair and loss loom large.

Several publications on the popular Christian book market have the phrases "All Things Work Together for Good" or "God Works All Things Together for Good" in their titles or subtitles. Typically, these books offer real-life testimonies on how tragic situations have led to spiritual lessons and renewed faith. The stories and reflections are moving and helpful, but the meaning of Romans 8:28 is simply assumed. When I leafed through one of these books, it occurred to me that even though Romans 8:28 appeared in the subtitle, the author never explained the verse in any of the chapters. Can we assume that the generally accepted meaning of the verse is what Paul intended?

Difficult crises often drive us to these two passages. Even so, I wonder if there is more to identifying with the conflicted soul of Romans 7. I wonder if there is more to seeking comfort in Romans 8 that things will turn out all right. When we cannot find anything of value in a seemingly meaningless tragedy, what are we saying when we declare that God makes all things work together for good? Do we really believe that what we are facing is included in "*all* things"? What kind of "good" are we supposed to expect from God and from the situation?

I think our popular interpretations of Romans 7:14-25 and 8:28 could use some adjusting to underscore both God's grander vision and God's loving provision for his children. By taking seriously Paul's train of thought in the first eight chapters of Romans, we will realize that these two passages are in fact closely related. They describe life on both sides of the death and resurrection of Jesus. Chapters 7 and 8 function as two halves of a diptych. Chapter 7 speaks of the futility of life of someone who is not yet regenerated and therefore still trapped under the power of sin. Chapter 8 portrays the life of the redeemed, empowered by the Spirit, who lives in victory and hope—both at the present time and in anticipation of God's promised future. In the rest of this chapter, I hope to walk the reader through Paul's theological and intellectual writing in the earlier chapters of Romans. In this way, we will not stumble upon 7:14-25 and 8:28, but place them along the progression of Paul's thought.

Paul and the Church in Rome

At the time of writing, Paul had not yet visited the church in Rome (1:11-13; 15:22-24), though he knew the people there (16:3-16). The church consisted of a mix of Jewish and Gentile Christians. Some of the Gentile Christians might have come to faith by way of Judaism, initially as God-fearers interested in the Jewish faith. Over time, the ratio between Jewish and Gentile Christians within the church might have shifted due to political circumstances.

According to one historical record, the ethnic composition of the Roman church changed as a result of an edict issued by Emperor Claudius around AD 49 to expel the Jews from Rome "because they were constantly rioting at the instigation of Chrestus" (Suetonius, *Life of Claudius*, 25.2). Modern scholars think "Chrestus" was a misrepresentation of "*Christos*" (Greek for "Christ"), and that the disturbances revolved around the claim that Jesus was the Christ, the Messiah. Many Jews, including Jewish

Christians, left Rome. Among them were Priscilla and Aquila, whom Paul met in Corinth (Acts 18:2). In the absence of Jewish Christians, the Roman church became mostly Gentile. Years later, Nero succeeded Claudius and lifted his edict. The return of the Jewish Christians to Rome and their re-assimilation into the Roman church might have led to disagreements as the community readjusted to having a mix of Jewish and Gentile believers (12:16-21; 14:1–15:13).

Writing to a church still trying to be unified, Paul stresses what the believers have in common. Whether Jew or Gentile, all are sinners and all need the gospel. God has provided to all people one solution for salvation through the death and resurrection of his Son. He also requires one response—faith in Jesus Christ. Regardless of their racial and spiritual starting points, the Christians in Rome are all children of God with the same Holy Spirit dwelling in them. Together they are headed for the same future glory. By emphasizing how much his readers have in common with one another, Paul draws their attention away from the differences and moves them toward a greater sense of theological and practical unity.

Finally, part of the challenge in reading and interpreting Romans lies in the range of possible translations of the same Greek word or phrase. This is especially difficult when dealing with loaded terms such as "righteousness," "faith," "faithfulness," or "works of the law." The variety in various modern English translations attests to the difficulty, as every translation reflects an interpretation and is not merely a word-for-word replacement of a word in Greek with its English equivalent. Therefore, even with the readings of Romans 7:14-25 and 8:28 presented below, it would be wise to leave room for alternate interpretations. That said, when conducted in a spirit of mutual respect, ongoing debates over the interpretation of Scripture can be intellectually stimulating and spiritually invigorating.

A Theocentric Gospel

Paul begins his long explanation of the gospel with a thesis statement: "For I am not ashamed of the gospel; it is the power of God for salvation to everyone who [believes], to the Jew first and also to the Greek. For in it the righteousness of God is revealed through the faithfulness [of Jesus] for [the purpose of] faith; as it is written, 'The righteous one will live by faith'" (1:16-17).

In ancient Mediterranean culture, the values of honor and shame dictated social status and the dynamics of human interaction. In this context,

Paul's words go beyond his not being embarrassed by the gospel; he is not self-conscious of how others might view him. Rather, having risked life and reputation to proclaim the good news of the crucified Christ, Paul is convinced that *God's* gospel is *God's* power manifesting *God's* righteousness! This is a theocentric gospel; it begins with God's initiative, followed by the outworking of God's plan of salvation. For a Jewish Christian and especially an ex-Pharisee like Paul, it is important that the creator God, the God of Abraham, is the same God and Father of the Lord Jesus Christ. Faith in Jesus is not received apart from the faith of his ancestors. In other words, Paul is not musing on a newly established religion. Rather, as a result of his encounter with Jesus on the road to Damascus (Acts 9:1-22), his life-changing experience forced him to rethink his inherited faith, of which he is still part, and his understanding of God's working among and through Israel. Although Jesus is not specifically mentioned in Romans 1:16-17, the opening verses of the letter provide a concise summary of "the gospel of God" in terms of the messianic mission of Jesus, the Davidic Son of God, who died on the cross and was raised from the dead (1:1-6).

Several other important points are introduced in this short thesis statement. On the one hand, the gospel of salvation is for everyone, Jew or Greek (Gentile) alike. On the other hand, within this inclusive salvation is something exclusive: the requirement of faith (*pistis* in the Greek). The translation offered above shows the nuances of the phrases: "For in [the gospel] the righteousness of God is revealed through the faithfulness [of Jesus] for [the purpose of] faith" (1:17). Jesus' faithfulness, shown in his obedience to go to the cross, allows us to understand and experience God's righteousness and become believers. Finally, the last key point is in the quotation of Habakkuk 2:4: "The righteous one will *live* by faith." The gospel requires a response that will lead to either eternal life or eternal death. In later chapters Paul will address the transformation believers experience in their identity and destiny as they leave the yoke of slavery and enter into a life of freedom in Christ.

Before we continue, it is worth pointing out that the challenge in translating from one language to another can be seen in 1:16-17. Not only does the Greek word *pistis* mean either faith or faithfulness, but the verb form, *pisteuō*, does not have an equivalent in the English (we do not say "I faith this"). Some translators make do with using the noun, "to have faith" (NRSV). Others go with the verb, "to believe," to keep the idea in the active voice. By using a synonym like "believe," the sequence of *pisteuonti*, *pisteōs*, *pistin*, and *pisteōs* in these two verses is broken up in the English translation, weakening the emphasis derived from the repetition. Even so, Paul's thesis statement introduces key concepts to which he will return repeatedly in the remainder of his letter. Gospel, salvation, power, righteousness, faith, and divine impartiality will factor into the explanation that follows.

Human Culpability and the Power of Sin

In the opening chapters of Romans, Paul makes a sweeping charge of human sinfulness that deserves God's wrath. The image of the ocean liner *Titanic* comes to mind: regardless of status, race, and origin, everyone is on the same sinking ship. All human beings are culpable before God. Paul charges first the Gentiles in chapter 1 and then the Jews in chapter 2. He is convinced that "there is no one who is righteous, not even one; there is no one who has understanding, there is no one who seeks God. All have turned aside, . . . since all have sinned and fall short of the glory of God" (3:11, 23).

The guilt of the Gentiles lies in their suppressing the truth that God is God (1:18). "Suppressing the truth" rules out the excuse that Gentiles are ignorant of the truth. They know but choose not to act on it. Creation alone gives sufficient demonstration of God's "eternal power and divine nature, invisible though they are" (1:20). Through observing the marvels of nature, it is impossible not to accept the created order as the works of a transcendent being. In short, Gentiles should have known better than to ignore God as God.

We may wonder whether it is fair for Paul to assume that Gentiles should know God even though they are not God's elect like the Jews. It may be helpful to note that Paul appeals to a mindset that is not exclusively Jewish. Ancient philosophers, such as the Stoic Epictetus among others, also employ the same logic. They say God—though not the God of Israel from their point of view—can be known through creation and the operation of the cosmos.

When Gentiles do not acknowledge the true God as God, ungodliness sets them on a vicious downward spiral of sins. Here Paul does not need an exhaustive list of sins to make his point. In Jewish thought, idolatry and sexual immorality are characteristic of pagan ungodliness. In the Old Testament, stubborn Israel is described as whoring after idols, an image that capitalizes on the worst of Gentile vices (Jer 3:1-5; Ezek 16:1-58). Instead of worshiping the true God and Creator, some Gentiles deify human rulers and heroes and bow down before images of animals, birds, and reptiles (1:23-25).

As a result of their apathy toward God, God's wrath descends upon the Gentiles in the form of inaction. Three times Paul repeats, "God gave them up in the lusts of their hearts to impurity. . . . God gave them up to degrading passions. . . . God gave them up to a debased mind and to things that should not be done" (1:24, 26, 28). When they push God to the point that even God lets go, there is no moral compass to bring them back. God allows their prideful and darkened minds to fuel their own decline. The Gentiles slide into an abyss of wickedness that feeds on its own evil (1:29-32).

Within this context of a sweeping outcry against Gentile sinfulness, Paul uses same-sex relationships as a case in point for sexual immorality: "Their women exchanged natural intercourse for unnatural, and in the same way also the men, giving up natural intercourse with women, were consumed with passion for one another. Men committed shameless acts with men and received in their own persons the due penalty for their error" (1:26-27). In 1:18-32, Paul's larger point is that idolatry and impiety have consequences. One of them is the warping of God's creative design of heterosexual relationships between males and females. Paul clearly objects to homosexuality, which is consistent with traditional Jewish and Old Testament thought (Lev 18:22). He says that much, but frankly not a whole lot more. These are two isolated verses taken from a larger context. On that basis, it would be difficult to construct an elaborate system of Pauline thought on the issue of homosexuality that addresses the multifaceted concerns of our modern era.

Space does not permit me to enter into a lengthy discussion of the marital rights of same-sex couples, the ordination of homosexual clergy, the origin of homosexual behavior as nature or nurture, and other related issues. I would, however, caution us to pay attention to the larger literary and historical backdrop of these two verses. May we hear Paul in *his* context and apply Scripture carefully? Contextual questions may include the following: Is it likely that Paul, writing two millennia ago to a particular congregation in Rome, had in mind the same questions we pose in the twenty-first century? Is homosexuality the key focus of Paul's entire discussion from verses 18 to 32, or is it simply an illustration of sexual immorality in the pagan world of his day? What does Paul mean by "natural" and "unnatural"? We should also consider ancient views and the prevalence of homosexual practices, including pederasty (men having sex with boys). It is difficult to imagine Paul, coming from a Jewish tradition, speaking positively about homosexual behavior. Still, we need not make him say something different from or beyond what he intended within the context of Romans 1, which was to use homosexual activity as an example of sinful behavior common in the first-century Gentile world.

Returning to the larger section of 1:18-25, we note that all Gentiles stand condemned. Because they have not given God his due honor, they are on the road to destruction. Even before the final judgment, God's wrath has already come upon them. While they have yet to suffer total annihilation on account of their godlessness, God has abandoned them to their own devices. They are trapped in an endless cycle of lies and spiritual dullness.

How about the Jews, God's chosen people? Do they fare better than the Gentiles? If the Gentiles should have known better from observing God's handiwork in nature, what can be said of the Jews who have the law (the Torah) to guide them? Certainly there is an advantage to being "entrusted with the oracles of God" (3:1-2). Unlike the Gentiles, the Jews are given a clear road map of life. From their dealings with one another to their relationship to God through worship, offertory regulations, and rites of sacrifice and circumcision, all of life is under God's law. Shouldn't that be rather straightforward?

Tragically, the Jews are as guilty as the Gentiles. Israel's track record in the Old Testament says as much. It is not enough to be hearers of the law if they are not also doers of the law (2:13). With the privilege of possessing the law comes the responsibility of obeying the law in order to reveal God to the unbelieving world. When the Jews take pride in the works of the law and set themselves over and above the "law-less" Gentiles, their failure to fulfill the law makes them even more liable than those who do not possess the law. In the end, the Jews who claim to be "a guide to the blind, a light to those who are in darkness, a corrector of the foolish, and a teacher of children" turn out to be none of these; they commit the very transgressions against which they preach (2:17-23). No wonder Paul laments over Israel's failure with words from Isaiah: "The name of God is blasphemed among the Gentiles because of you" (2:24; cf. Isa 52:5). At least in Isaiah God's name was blasphemed by Gentiles who oppressed his people. Here in Romans God's people themselves commit the blasphemy when their moral and spiritual failures are on display for the world to see.

Therefore, with or without the law, both Jews and Gentiles are declared unrighteous before a righteous God. Behind their repeated infractions against God lies a real culprit. Paul identifies the force behind all human sinning as a strong sinister power that leads to death: "All, both Jews and Greeks, are under the power of sin" (3:9). Without exception, fallen humanity finds itself tight in sin's grip. Nowhere in Romans does Paul reflect on where the power of sin comes from or who is responsible for its existence. It just is. Neither does he equate the devil with the power of sin. Paul takes seriously human responsibility for moral and spiritual immorality. He leaves no room for anyone to make an excuse out of the quip, "The devil made me do it."

God's Impartial Judgment

Without divine intervention, the human condition leads to only one thing—death and eternal separation from God. By their own strength and will, fallen human beings do not have the moral and spiritual goodness to overcome the power of sin. In this regard, the image of slavery is fitting. Jews and Gentiles alike are enslaved or under the mastery of sin. From the position of powerlessness, sinful humanity needs to be redeemed and delivered by God in order to be reconciled to God. The only option, aside from eternal extermination, is to be a passive recipient of God's saving grace.

Can't God simply cancel judgment and show mercy? Not if God's integrity is to be maintained. God manifests his wrath because he is just and true to his word, his holiness, and his righteousness. If God were unpredictable regarding his warning to judge, why should anyone believe that he would be predictable in his promise to save? Consistency is an expression of God's faithfulness, and if it is so with his blessings, it should be so with his warnings as well. Paul maintains that God "will repay according to each one's deeds" (2:6), "glory and honor and peace for everyone who does good" (2:10), and "anguish and distress for everyone who does evil" (2:9). Any seeming delay of judgment is not a sign of God wavering in his response to wickedness, but a demonstration of his compassion and patience in order that some might still repent (2:4-5).

When judgment day comes, Jews and Gentiles will either be glorified or condemned in accordance with their deeds, "for God shows no partiality" (2:9-11). Although the Gentiles do not have the Torah, their conscience and sense of right and wrong will serve as a standard against which their actions will be measured (2:14-16). For Jews who have the Torah, they will be judged by the law. Unless they prove themselves obedient to the law, their circumcision—a symbol of their privileged status that sets them apart from the Gentiles—is of no value. The reverse is true as well. Uncircumcised Gentiles, by their obedience to God even though they are not aware of the specific statutes of the Torah, are treated as though they were circumcised and hence acceptable to God (2:25-29). In short, circumcision, an outward mark of one's identity in God's people, is meaningful only if the inner reality of the heart attests to it. As Paul writes in his letter to the Galatians, "For in Christ Jesus neither circumcision nor uncircumcision counts for anything, the only thing that counts is faith working through love" (Gal 5:6). In the end, circumcision of the heart matters more than the physical circumcision of the flesh.

The reality is that all human beings will find themselves condemned because no person is righteous before God (3:9-19). Something needs to be done to alter the doomed inevitability of eternal death. Since human beings are incapable of saving themselves, God intervenes with his gospel of salvation. He offers a way out through the death and resurrection of his Son. As we shall see in the next section, the gospel of God is the power of God in action. God's solution to the human dilemma fulfills his justice, reconciles human beings to him, and definitively destroys the power of sin.

God's "Righteousizing" Solution in Christ Jesus

The most succinct statement in Romans of God's solution to the human predicament is found in chapter 3. This passage is so important that it is worth quoting in full:

> But now, apart from the law, the <u>righteousness</u> of God has been disclosed, and is attested by the law and the prophets, the <u>righteousness</u> of God through the **faithfulness** of Jesus Christ (or **faith** in Jesus Christ) for all who **believe**. For there is no distinction, since all have sinned and fall short of the glory of God; they are now <u>justified</u> by his grace as a gift, through the redemption that is in Christ Jesus; whom God put forward as a sacrifice of atonement (Greek: *hilastērion*) by his blood, effective through **faith**. He did this to show his <u>righteousness</u>, because in his divine forbearance he had passed over the sins previously committed; it was to prove at the present time that he himself is <u>righteous</u> and that he <u>justifies</u> the one who has **faith** in Jesus. (3:21-26)

First of all, note the words that are underlined and boldfaced. Here are two examples of how the English translation slightly obscures the repetition in the original language. The underlined words "righteousness" (*dikaiosunē*), "righteous" (*dikaion*), and "justifies/justified" (*dikaioō*) all share the same Greek root; so do the boldfaced words "faithfulness" (*pistis*), "believe" (*pisteuō*), and "faith" (*pistis*).

The terms "justification" (*dikaiosunē*) and "justify" (*dikaioō*) tend to convey a legal or forensic meaning to English speakers, conjuring up the image of a court of law, where the accused is either found guilty or innocent of the alleged crime. While this use of the *dikaio-* word group is certainly found in the Septuagint, the Greek translation of the Hebrew Scriptures (e.g., Isa 43:26), God's *dikaiosune* is also introduced in relation to his covenantal faithfulness, salvation, and vindication:

> My righteousness speedily draws nigh,
> and my salvation shall go forth as light. (Isa 51:5)

> Thou shall quicken me, O LORD, for Thy name's sake;
> In Thy righteousness Thou shall bring my soul out of affliction.
> (Ps 143:11)

Therefore, when Paul speaks of God's righteousness or justification, he sees not only a God who is in the right and judges accordingly, but also one who keeps his promise of salvation in order to restore the broken relationship between him and his people. As such, God's righteousness is not static but dynamic. It is more than an attribute of God. It shows God in action—justifying, rectifying, "righteousizing"—making right what has gone wrong, and in the process providing a way to reconcile humankind to him.

What does the "righteousizing action" of God entail? According to Paul, God's righteousness comes in the form of a gift. A gift, by definition, is an expression of pure grace. It can neither be earned nor bought. God's gift of salvation is received by trusting in the giver's power and believing in the gift's effectiveness in combating the power of sin. Two Old Testament images further explain how the gift "works": one is redemption; the other is atonement.

Redemption is an economic concept that refers to the buying back of slaves. Since they lived as slaves in Egypt and exiles in Babylon, the painful reality of slavery is deeply embedded in Israel's history and psyche. Now all of humankind, Jews and Gentiles, are said to be enslaved by the power of sin. Unless they are delivered by a power outside themselves, they will remain forever trapped and doomed to eternal death. When Paul writes, "all are now justified by [God's] grace as a gift, through the redemption that is in Christ Jesus" (3:24), he is making the point that Jesus Christ is the means by which sinners gain freedom from slavery under the power of sin. This is a crucial point and it is important to leave it simple. Speculating on whether God had to pay the devil "ransom money" in the form of Jesus' life to buy back sinners would take the image beyond what seems to be intended in this context. After all, Paul gives no hint of any such transaction. In our eagerness to make a text come alive, we need to take care not to embellish details that distract rather than clarify.

The other image is found in the next verse: "[Jesus Christ] . . . whom God put forward as a *hilastērion* by his blood" (3:25). *Hilastērion* is the Greek word for the cover of the ark of the covenant. According to the Old Testament, once a year, on the Day of Atonement, the high priest atones for his own sins and the sins of Israel. He sprinkles the blood of the sacrificial animal on the cover of the ark, also known as "the mercy seat," to consecrate the holy of holies (Lev 16:14-16). Paul uses the image of this ceremony to explain the significance of Jesus' death on the cross. Without locking down the metaphor too tightly, we are to understand that Jesus died on behalf of God's people and his death atoned for their sins. Even the identity of Jesus with the cover of the ark (*hilastērion*) is not meant to be entirely rigid. We are to think of Jesus not only as the locus of divine forgiveness (the mercy seat), but also consider his death as a sin offering producing atonement (as with the blood of the sacrificial animal). Because Jesus' death fulfills the just requirement of God in response to sins, "[God] had passed over the sins previously committed" (3:25), and, by implication, all sins yet to be committed as well.

The general sense of Paul's description of Jesus as *hilastērion* is not difficult to grasp, though a precise translation is a challenge. Among various English versions, the rendering of *hilastērion* ranges from "sacrifice of atonement" (NRSV, NIV), "expiation" (NAB), "means of expiating sins" (NEB), to "propitiation" (KJV, ASV, NASB). All these translations are interpretations of Paul's language regarding the "function" of Jesus' death on the cross. They reflect what the translators believe Jesus' death actually does for those who put their trust in its role for their salvation. "Sacrifice of atonement" identifies Jesus with the sin offering in the Old Testament sacrificial system. "Expiation" is related to atonement, pointing to something that wipes away sin, the cause of God's wrath. But this is still somewhat imprecise, for what does it mean to "wipe away sin"? "Propitiation" is more problematic because it implies the turning away or reduction of the intensity of God's wrath. The issue here is not God's wrath *per se*, as though a "wrathful" God must then be hot-tempered and unpredictable like the gods of the pagans. Paul has already argued in chapter 1 that God's wrath is God's response to human wickedness because he is holy and just, not because he enjoys "flying off the handle." Therefore, to relegate God to the ranks of fickle pagan deities and view Jesus' death as a means to appease an angry God are both misleading. Among these options, "sacrifice of atonement" and "atoning sacrifice" seem to reflect the Old Testament background of Paul's image most directly, even though we should be aware that none of these phrases translates the Greek word *hilastērion* literally.

Pulling the different strands together, we can now see the creativity of God's solution to the human dilemma. In one fell swoop, God addresses both the trespasses and sinful deeds that individuals have committed against him, using the image of atonement with Jesus as the sin offering, as well as the power of sin that enslaves all humankind, using the image of redemption.

First, in response to trespasses and sinful deeds, God's justice must be upheld. Human disobedience will ultimately answer to God's final judgment. Without breaking his own rules, God provided a solution that maintained his integrity while at the same time kept his promise of salvation. As Paul writes, "God proves his love for us in that while we still were sinners Christ died for us" (5:8); God did not wait for all humankind to qualify, so to speak, for forgiveness. He "put forward [Jesus Christ] as a sacrifice of atonement" (3:25), so that "at the right time Christ died for the ungodly" (5:6). Paul cannot stress enough the divine plan: God came up with the solution; God provided the atoning sacrifice in his Son; God determined the right time; and God made sure that his justice and faithfulness were not compromised in the process. Nevertheless, this "righteousizing" action of God was brought to fruition through "the faithfulness of Jesus Christ" (3:22, 25), whose unwavering resolve to obey his Father's will took him all the way to the cross (cf. Phil 2:6-11; Mark 14:36).

Second, God must provide a greater power to subdue the power of sin. This is achieved by Jesus' redemptive action on the cross, freeing humankind from the bondage of sin. Paul explains in Romans 5 how Jesus reversed the deadly course set in motion by Adam's sin. Adam and Jesus are representative figures of the old age and the new age. Those who belong to the old age are aligned with Adam, trapped under the dominion of sin. Those who belong to Jesus are people of the new age, living a life characterized by righteousness and grace. Between the old age and the new age, the death and resurrection of Jesus comprise the watershed event that makes possible a person's transfer from a destiny of condemnation and death to one of justification and life.

Evoking Adam brings to mind the story of the fall in Genesis 2–3, at the end of which the punishment for sinning against God was death. This is Paul's starting point. He does not inquire into the origin of sin or how sin came to be in the first place. Rather, he asserts that "sin came into the world through one man, and death came through sin, and so death spread to all because all have sinned" (5:12). The power of sin gained a foothold in Adam, and in the same way, it holds sway over every single human being since Adam, even if the sins committed may not be the same as Adam's first transgression (5:14). Without God's intervention, the universal dominion of sin results in universal death. At issue for Paul here is not whether it is fair that all of humankind is implicated by the disobedience of Adam and his sin. Rather, the sins of humankind are already evidence of the power of sin at work. Paul is much more interested in how this vicious cycle can be interrupted once and for all by Jesus' work of grace.

Jesus is like Adam in that they are both figures whose action implicates those who follow suit. At the same time, Jesus is not like Adam because he reversed the consequence of Adam's action. The following verses capture both the continuity and the discontinuity between Jesus and Adam: "Therefore just as one man's trespass led to condemnation for all, so one man's act of righteousness leads to justification and life for all. For just as by the one man's disobedience the many were made sinners, so by the one man's obedience the many will be made righteous" (5:18-19). Jesus powerfully and overwhelmingly reversed the course set by Adam. The benefits of Jesus' work of grace far outweigh the havoc wreaked by Adam:

> For if the many died through the one man's trespass, *much more surely* have the grace of God and the free gift in the grace of the one man, Jesus Christ, abounded for many. (5:15)

> If, because of the one man's trespass, death exercised dominion through that one, *much more surely* will those who receive the abundance of grace and the free gift of righteousness exercise dominion in life through the one man, Jesus Christ. (5:17)

How, then, is the power of sin broken? This entails not only the cross, but the resurrection as well. Had Jesus died and stayed dead like the animal of the sin offering, the power of sin would persist, and atoning sacrifices would still have to be made for transgression after transgression, year after year. By raising Jesus from the dead, God shows that his power is stronger than the power of sin: "Christ . . . will never die again; death no longer has dominion over him. The death he died, he died to sin, once for all; but the life he lives, he lives to God" (6:9; cf. Heb 7:27; 9:12). Those who believe in the atoning value of the death of Jesus on their behalf are forgiven of their trespasses and at the same time forever redeemed from the bondage of sin.

Thus far we have not broached the subject of the appropriate response to God's offer of grace, which is the focus of the next section. By separating what God has already done on his end and what we are invited to do on ours, I hope to underscore the point that God's gift in Jesus Christ is undeserved and divinely initiated, so that there is no basis for boasting when it comes to salvation, whether in the works of the law or in any other form of human achievement.

Faith in Jesus Christ and Radical Transformation

Back in chapter 1, Paul's thesis statement is that "the gospel . . . is the power of God for salvation to everyone who has faith" (1:16). Throughout the ensuing chapters, he repeatedly indicates that the proper human response to God's "righteousizing" action is "faith in Jesus" (3:22, 26), so that "justified by faith, we have peace with God through our Lord Jesus Christ" (5:1; cf. 3:28).

What kind of faith is Paul referring to? In chapter 4, Paul uses the example of Abraham as the prototype of the faith that would allow a believer to be counted as righteous before God. Since Paul appeals to the chronological time line in the book of Genesis to construct his argument, let's review the chain of events.

Abraham, then still known as Abram, was seventy-five years old when God called him out of Haran with the promise, "I will make of you a great nation, and I will bless you, and make your name great, so that you will be a blessing" (Gen 12:1-4). Since then the promise of countless descendants for Abram was reaffirmed when God compared his offspring to the dust of the earth and the stars in the sky (Gen 13:14-16; 15:5). Abram's response was simple yet profound: "And he believed the LORD; and the LORD reckoned it to him as righteousness" (Gen 15:6). It was no small feat to have to wait for another quarter of a century for the arrival of the child of promise. When Abram was ninety-nine years old, God once again reiterated the promise that he would make Abram "exceedingly numerous," and sealed that promise with a formal covenant. Moreover, God changed Abram's name to Abraham and established the rite of circumcision as a sign of the covenant between God and Abraham's children forever (Gen 17:1-22). A year later, when Abraham was a hundred years old, Isaac was born (Gen 21:1-5).

Without repeating the entire story, which is likely familiar to the Christians in Rome, Paul hones in on the point of the Genesis narrative where God declared Abraham righteous on account of his faith. Abraham had unwavering trust that God would bring to pass what he had promised. Abraham's faith was all the more commendable given his and Sarah's old age and barrenness. But "hope against hope, he believed that he would become the father of many nations" (4:18).

The crucial point for Paul is that Abraham exercised his faith *before, and not after, his circumcision.* This means that circumcision was not the requirement, but the confirmation, of Abraham's righteous status before God. The requirement was pure faith and simple trust. This distinction is not merely a chronological detail, especially when circumcision is the key identity marker that sets the Jews, the covenant people of God, apart from the Gentiles. Since Abraham was justified by faith while he was not yet circumcised, Paul's logic is that any uncircumcised Gentile who trusts God with the same kind of faith will also be justified by God. As for the Jews who are circumcised and call Abraham their father, they, too, will be justified, not because of their physical circumcision, but because they take after their ancestor and come to God with a simple trust in God's faithfulness (4:9-12). In this way, Abraham can truly be deemed the "father of many nations" (4:17), certainly in terms of physical descendants, but even more so in terms of spiritual descendants. For both Jews and Gentiles, the reason of justification is the same; it is faith and not ancestry (4:16; cf. Luke 3:6-8).

Once again, the note of God's impartiality is struck. Jews and Gentiles begin as equally guilty before God. God provides for all the same solution in Jesus Christ and demands from all the same type of faith as that of Abraham. This faith has nothing to do with individual performance, because the bodies of Abraham and Sarah were "as good as dead" (4:19). Yet Abraham believed in a God "who gives life to the dead and calls into existence the things that do not exist" (4:17). This same God, argues Paul, will also bring life out of death, first of all in the resurrection of Jesus Christ, and later in the future resurrection of all believers (6:5).

In no uncertain terms Paul uses a number of images to express the radical transformation in a person's identity and destiny. This change happens when one is rendered righteous before God through believing in Jesus as the atoning sacrifice for one's sins. Once enemies because of sin, Christians now enjoy peace and reconciliation in their relationship with God (5:1, 10-11). Paul depicts believers as people freed from the power of sin and realigned under the "benevolent slavery" of God. While the language of slavery may seem off-putting, Paul's point is that human beings are not autonomous no matter how much they would like to think they are. There are only two options of existence, and they cannot coexist: living under the domination of sin or under the domination of grace (5:21; 6:14). Freedom from the power of sin is essentially a transfer—both spiritual and ethical—from being "slaves of sin" to becoming "slaves of obedience" and "slaves of righteousness" (6:6-7, 16-18). Under the influence of the power of sin, a sinner's body serves as "[an instrument] of wickedness," full of impurity that leads to condemnation. But freedom from sin results in justification and a life of sanctification, so that the body now functions as "[an instrument] of righteousness" (5:16, 18; 6:13, 19). As for their final destiny, believers will be spared from final death and will enter eternal life with God (5:17; 6:11, 23).

Thus far, we have followed Paul's explanation of God's plan of salvation in terms of why it is needed, what God has done through Jesus, and what the implications are for those who believe. It is not difficult to imagine Gentile Christians, for example, those in the Roman church, fitting into this schema as they journey from paganism to believing in Jesus. The trajectory for Jewish Christians (and Paul is among them), however, is less straightforward. If the Jews have the Torah, why do they still need Jesus? Isn't following the law enough for eternal life? For Paul, the issue of the law is important because it defines Jewish identity as God's covenantal people and regulates all aspects of Jewish life. As a Jewish Christian and a Christian Jew, if Paul concludes that justification by faith is *apart from the law*, then he needs to clarify the place of the law in relation to the gospel of salvation through Jesus Christ. Put differently, what does it mean for Paul when Jesus claims that he comes "not to abolish but to fulfill" the law (Matt 5:17)? In what way is the law put in its rightful place—yet not discarded—as a result of what Jesus has accomplished on the cross? A discussion of the role of the law will also provide a natural transition to our reading of Romans 7:14-25. To this we now turn.

The Place of the Torah and the Conflicted Self of Romans 7:14-25

Paul knows and loves the law. After all, he is the student of Gamaliel, one of the most famous rabbis of his day (Acts 5:34; 22:3). In his letter to the Philippians, Paul describes his life before his encounter with the risen Jesus: "as to the law, a Pharisee; . . . as to righteousness under the law, blameless"

(Phil 3:5-6). Even though Paul says he regards all his prior achievements as loss in comparison to knowing Jesus (Phil 3:8), there is no hint that because he has become a Christian he is now anti-law. Yet in Romans and Galatians we see how Paul puts the law in its proper perspective in the wake of the Messiah's coming.

To the Jews "entrusted with the oracles of God" (3:2), the law is a gift and a privilege. It is God's providence for his people, not a burden on them. The Jews have "in the law the embodiment of knowledge and truth" (2:20). The written law in the five books of Moses and the oral law passed down by the rabbis instruct the Jews to live in a way that reflects their status as God's chosen people. Adherence to the law, however meticulous it may appear to outsiders, is not meant to be a burden for the Jews but a response of covenantal faithfulness on their part. After all, when asked to identify the greatest commandment, Jesus' twofold answer, loving God and loving neighbor, comes straight out of the Old Testament (Matt 22:36-40; cf. Deut 6:4; Lev 19:18). Therefore, as a Christian, Paul continues to affirm the value of the law: "Do we then overthrow the law by this faith? By no means! On the contrary, we uphold the law" (3:31); "the law is holy, and the commandment is holy and just and good" (7:9); "I agree that the law is good" (7:16); "I delight in the law of God in my inmost being" (7:22).

In addition to these positive statements about the law, Paul also speaks of the law in relation to sin and death: "You are not under law but under grace" (6:14-15); "But now we are discharged from the law, dead to that which held us captive, so that we are slaves not under the old written code but in the new life of the Spirit" (7:6); "I was once alive apart from the law, but when the commandments came, sin revived and I died, and the very commandment that promised life proved to be death to me" (7:9-10). Yet despite the negative depiction of the law and even its association with sin and death, Paul insists that law and sin are not to be collapsed into one: "What then should we say? That the law is sin? By no means!" (7:7).

The key to unlocking this seemingly perplexing contradiction is found in two ways: (1) in Paul's view of the *function* of the law in light of the historical time line of God's plan of salvation and (2) in the *manipulation* of the law by the power of sin that makes the saving action of Jesus necessary. The law is a set of standards set by God that defines transgressions: "If it had not been for the law, I would not have known sin. I would not have known what it is to covet if the law had not said, 'You shall not covet'" (7:7-8). Other statements in Romans make the same point: "Sin was in the world before the law, but sin is not reckoned when there is no law" (5:13); "the law brings wrath; but where there is no law, neither is there violation" (4:15). As the law makes sin more easily identifiable, it also makes people more accountable for their actions.

The logic is not difficult to grasp. A sign that says "Speed Limit: 65 miles per hour" indicates the speed beyond which a driver violates the traffic law. Without such a law, there is neither accountability nor consequence for reckless driving. Likewise, with the giving of the law at Sinai, the standard for measuring human motives and behavior is made clear, so that shortfalls are more easily identified and prominently displayed. When Paul uses the language "but law came in, with the result that the trespass multiplied," (5:20), he is not saying that all was well between Adam and Moses. Instead, he means that the awareness and effect of sinfulness are made more concrete by the introduction of the law. Thus in Galatians Paul views the law as having a pedagogical (educational) function, that "the law was our disciplinarian (*paidagōgos* in Greek) until Christ came" (Gal 3:24, NRSV). Other translations of *paidagōgos* include "tutor" (NKJV) and "custodian" (RSV), which offer slightly different emphases, but the general idea is the same.

If the law is intended for the positive functions of guidance and accountability, how can something so life-giving become so entangled with the death-dealing power of sin? What role does the law play in the human dilemma? Paul's reasoning highlights the treachery of the power of sin: "While we were living in the flesh, our sinful passions, aroused by the law, were at work in our members to bear fruit for death" (7:5). With the example of Adam's fall just two chapters earlier in chapter 5, the reader might catch an allusion to it here in chapter 7. The serpent cast doubt on Adam and Eve's belief in God's warning not even to touch the tree of the knowledge of good and evil, let alone eat of its fruit. He goaded them into taking the forbidden fruit, which led to their banishment from the garden with the sentence of death (Gen 3:1-24). Sin uses the good boundaries of God to arouse a person's sinful passions to do exactly the opposite, that is, to test and ultimately break the boundaries. We do not need to observe the behavior of little children to admit that we, too, sometimes flirt with forbidden territory. Without a rule in place, we probably would not have thought of doing anything wrong. But once we are aware of the rule, we begin to wonder what it would be like to stretch it, get around it, or break it. This is why Paul identifies sin as the powerful instigator for people to disobey, with deadly results: "Sin, seizing an opportunity in the commandment, deceived me and through it killed me" (7:11). In other words, sin's true color is revealed as "sinful beyond measure" because it does its damage in underhanded ways. It twists what is good in order to get a response that embodies its sinister agenda (7:13). With this appreciation of how sin functions as an evil power, we arrive at Romans 7:14-25, the description of a person trapped between the will to obey God's law and the propensity to do evil.

Scholars debate the identity of "I" in this passage. Is it Paul or a representative figure? This matter is actually of secondary concern, for the two are not incompatible. Paul can envision himself in the description but also maintains that others share this experience. A more important interpretive issue is whether "the wretched man" depicts the struggle of a Christian or of a Jewish person who is unable to follow God's law in spite of his best intentions. I argue for the latter as the appropriate lens through which to consider this passage.

Verse 14 comes immediately after Paul reveals sin's manipulation of the law to bring about evil (7:7-13). The "I" is the same "I" who knows that the law says one should not covet, but in whom "sin, seizing an opportunity in the commandment, produced . . . all kinds of covetousness" (7:8). The description of 7:14-25 characterizes a Jew, like Paul in his pre-Christian days, who wants to obey the law but falters under the power of sin. One feels the frustration and tension in this confession, as "the wretched man" names his inner contradictions: "I do not do what I want, but I do the very thing that I hate" (7:15); "I do not do the good I want, but the evil I do not want is what I do" (7:19). Even when he knows full well that "the law is spiritual" (7:14) and that he "[delights] in the law of God in [his] inmost self" (7:22), he is pulled away from the law of God by the law of sin. The metaphors of battle and slavery show that the struggle is ferocious: "I see in my members another law at war with the law of my mind, making me captive to the law of sin that dwells in my members" (7:23); "with my mind I am a slave to the law of God, but with my flesh I am a slave to the law of sin" (7:25). Indeed, the man cannot have two masters, and in his current condition, the law of sin has the upper hand. Why is that? Because the power of sin lives within him: "Now if I do what I do not want, I agree that the law is good. But in fact it is no longer I that do it, but sin that dwells within me" (7:16-18, 20, 23). When sin is an indwelling force within a person, it is ready to pounce at any time: "When I want to do what is good, evil lies close at hand" (7:21). Once sin has the upper hand on the person, "the mind that is set on the flesh is hostile to God; it does not submit to God's law—indeed it cannot, and those who are in the flesh cannot please God" (8:7-8). So even though the delight of the heart is for the law of God, the power of sin makes it impossible for even the most law-loving Jew to keep the commandments perfectly. If the Jews, with the gift of God's law, cannot overcome sin, what hope is there for Gentiles, such as those described in Romans 1, who do not have the law in the first place?

The problem with the law is not that it has become obsolete and irrelevant upon the coming of Jesus. Neither did God make a mistake in giving the law to a disobedient people. The problem lies in the fact that human beings, even the covenant people of God, *simply cannot* keep the law perfectly enough to be deemed righteous before God. Since the time of Adam, the power of sin enslaves everyone, and no amount of good intentions can overcome its control. While salvation might be sought with perfect adherence to the law, in reality it has never been and will never be the case for any fallen human being.

The shift for Paul, as he moves from Jew to Christian Jew/Jewish Christian, lies in the realization that the law ultimately does not have the power to save. Only Jesus is the means of salvation: "For God has done what the law, weakened by the flesh, could not do: by sending his own Son in the likeness of sinful flesh, and to deal with sin, he condemned sin in the flesh, so that the just requirement of the law might be fulfilled in us, who walk not according to the flesh but according to the Spirit" (8:2-4).

Since sin targets human beings "in the flesh" with ungodly impulses and passions, Jesus, who comes "in the likeness of sinful flesh," is essential to the plan of salvation. He fights sin on its own turf. Only Jesus' bodily resurrection, following his bodily death, can defeat the power of sin that holds sway over humanity. Thus for those who are united with Jesus in his death through baptism, their "body of sin" is destroyed, and in the future they may be raised to new life just as he was (6:3-6).

Even as God's "righteousizing" action operates apart from the law, it manages to have the law fulfilled in those who believe in Jesus. What does it mean for the "just requirement of the law [to be] fulfilled in us" (8:4)? The answer lies in the second half of verse 4: "us" refers to those who "walk not according to the flesh but according to the Spirit." Without the empowerment of the Holy Spirit, it is impossible for anyone to follow the law and please God (8:5-8). The power of the Holy Spirit, given only to Christians who believe in Jesus Christ and have made the transfer from the old to the new self, is God's own power that raised Jesus from the dead. Imagine replacing the power of sin with this benevolent power. Imagine the moral and spiritual transformation this can bring to those who believe!

This hope of new life is out of reach for those still trapped under the bondage of sin, including those who attempt to attain salvation by doing the works of the law. Jesus is the only way out. The depth of despair in the heart-wrenching cry, "Wretched man that I am! Who will rescue me from this body of death?" (7:24) is matched by the depth of gratitude in the answer, "Thanks be to God through Jesus Christ our Lord!" (7:25). When Paul declares, "There is therefore now no condemnation for those who are in Christ Jesus" (8:1), the hopelessness of chapter 7 (a life without Christ and plagued by sin) gives way to the newness of chapter 8 (a life with Christ and empowered by the Spirit). Moving from Romans 7 to 8, there is a sense of expansion in horizon. The suffocation and restrictiveness of chapter 7 give way to the hope and expansiveness of chapter 8, in which Paul paints with broad, carefree strokes a grand vision of God's love in Christ Jesus that encompasses the entire cosmos.

The Cosmic Vision of Romans 8:28

On the time line of salvation, Jesus has *already* come and fulfilled the work of salvation by his death and resurrection. The grand finale into the new age of eternity, however, has *not yet* taken place. How does the spiritual reality of a redeemed life affect the practical realities of an earthly existence sandwiched between the "already" and the "not yet"? If physical death and suffering do not vanish even after a person professes faith in Christ, what does change?

The indwelling of the Holy Spirit affirms for believers that they are free from sin and accepted into God's family even now. It bears witness to their status as adopted children of God. They can now address God as "Abba! Father!" On the one hand, their adoption is decided. As co-heirs with Jesus, believers will one day share in his glory (8:14-17). On the other hand, Paul speaks of an adoption that will take place in the future: "We groan inwardly while we wait for adoption, the redemption of our bodies" (8:23). These two are not contradictory; instead, they reflect life between the "already" and the "not yet."

Clearly for Paul, the Christian life on earth already operates under the new empowerment of God's Spirit, since freedom from sin has already been achieved. Paul exhorts his readers not to "let sin exercise dominion in [their] mortal bodies, . . . for sin will have no dominion over [them] since [they] are not under law but under grace" (6:12, 14). Yet Christians still live inside mortal and decaying bodies. To live between the "already" and the "not yet," Paul approaches life in the time-bound and earth-bound present through the lens of God's promised future. This future is characterized by peace, righteousness, and glory. Reflecting on his suffering for the gospel, Paul stresses this "eschatological/end-time" view when writing to the church in Corinth:

> So we do not lose heart. Even though our outer nature is wasting away, our inner nature is being renewed day by day. For this slight momentary affliction is preparing us for an eternal weight of glory beyond all measure, because we look not at what can be seen but at what cannot be seen; for what can be seen is temporary, but what cannot be seen is eternal. (2 Cor 4:16-18)

In like manner, in Romans 8 Paul contemplates the future glory in God's eternal presence to keep his present sufferings in perspective:

> I consider that the sufferings of this present time are not worth comparing with the glory about to be revealed to us. . . . For in hope we were saved. Now hope that is seen is not hope. For who hopes for what is seen? But if we hope for what we do not see, we wait for it with patience. (8:18, 24-25)

Just as Paul is realistic about the human condition in need of salvation, he acknowledges the difficulties of this life. Earlier in the letter he speaks of the "benefits" of suffering as a training ground for endurance, character, and hope (5:3-5). Now he assures his readers that even when they find themselves in such a state of distress that they no longer know how to pray, the Holy Spirit and Jesus himself intercede on their behalf before their loving Father (8:26-27, 34).

As Paul approaches the climax of his long explanation of God's plan of salvation, he moves beyond the human realm and declares that even creation as a whole "was subjected to futility, . . . groaning in labor pains until now" (8:20, 22). Because of the fall, the entire created order is implicated. But when God saves, nothing is left behind. The rest of creation will also be "set free from its bondage to decay and will obtain the freedom of the glory of the children of God" (8:21).

As Paul approaches the climax of his long explanation of God's plan of salvation, Paul writes this famous verse: "We know that God makes all things work together for good for those who love God, who are called according to his purpose" (8:28). In some ancient manuscripts, the action of God is implied in the Greek, so other English translations read, "We know that all things work together for good for those who love God." Either way, God is the subject of the action. He is the one working things for good, since things cannot "work themselves." Given the context, this verse promises that in the end, when the plan of salvation finally reaches its grand conclusion, God will reconcile all things so that those who love him will receive the full benefit.

The next two verses expound on what it means to be "called according to [God's] purpose" with a fivefold progression—"those whom he foreknew he also predestined to be confirmed to the image of his Son, . . . he also called, . . . he also justified, . . . he also glorified" (8:29-30). It is unlikely that the doctrine of predestination versus free will is in view here. Rather, the string of verbs emphasizes the purpose and sovereignty of God who designs and executes his plan of salvation as he sees fit.

The conviction of God's love in Romans 8:28 allows us to trust that God's "righteousizing action" extends beyond what we can perceive and absorb in the here and now, especially in the midst of present disappointments and contradictions. When we say, "We know that God works all things together for good for those who love God," we make a *faith claim* about the final reality at the end of time. This is no wobbly hope that perhaps, just this once, for this situation, things might turn out the way we hope. Instead, "God makes all things work together for good" is a declaration of confidence in God's divine purpose for the universe. It is much more powerful and far-reaching than what we normally allow it to be in popular usage.

When we use Romans 8:28 to express a hope or prayer for a difficult situation, we get a little nervous. What if God does not intervene? Must I find something redeeming the tragedy so I can call it "good" and claim that God makes all things work out "for good"? Does God's inaction have to do with whether I love God enough or not? I don't think these questions are helpful. God's reputation does not rise or fall according to what we think of his response to our lives. Rather, God's saving purposes transcend the here and now and reach into the eternal future. *This* assurance leads Paul to declare, "God works all things together for good for those who love God." Paul does not need everything to "work out right" in his life. His sufferings are a case in point (2 Cor 4:8-12; 6:4-10). Through it all, he can say to his Roman readers, "I consider that the sufferings of this present time are not worth comparing with the glory about to be revealed to us" (8:18; cf. 8:35-37; 2 Cor 4:16-18). His attitude toward the present—whatever his circumstance—is informed and transformed by his trust in God's promised future.

Armed with unwavering trust in God's love for all creation, Paul brings his long discussion to a close. In the broadest terms, he includes everything in the universe—death, life, angels, rulers, things present, things to come, powers, height, depth, anything else in all creation—to affirm that none of these will ever come between God's love and his redeemed universe (8:38-39). With this conviction, all the sufferings in life may be put in their proper place.

Conclusion

Paul's presentation of the gospel in the first eight chapters of Romans is breathtaking. By leveling the playing field for both Jews and Gentiles before a God who shows no partiality in judgment and in salvation, Paul makes plain that justification is by faith apart from the law. Only the sacrifice of Jesus can destroy the power of sin and reconcile believers to God. Jesus' death and resurrection, and his gift of the Holy Spirit as a power that resides within believers, enable believers to live righteously before God. They do this not by their own strength but with the help of the Holy Spirit. Only in this manner are the "just requirements" of the law fulfilled (8:4), allowing Paul to uphold the value of the law without making it do more than what it is intended to do.

I have tried to illustrate that chapters 7 and 8 of Romans should be read together, showing what life is like before and after regeneration in Jesus. More specifically, chapter 7 depicts the "Jewish" condition without Christ. Our first passage of interest, 7:14-25, portrays the tortured soul of a Jewish person, trapped between loyalty to God's law and slavery under the law of sin. The vicious cycle of chapter 7 is broken by the gospel of Jesus Christ. Then life in the Spirit in chapter 8 is fully open to experiencing God's redemptive future. Our second passage of interest, 8:28, "that God works all things together for good for those who love God," provides a vision of what that future looks like. While God's purposes may not always match our idea of "goodness" on this side of eternity between the "already" and the "not yet," by faith we trust that God is for us and not against us.

Imagine a tapestry: God sees the whole design from above, noting where every color or thread belongs; we see the messy underside, knots and all. In the end, what matters is the divine perspective, especially when the picture is planned and woven in love. Indeed, "[the God] who did not withhold his own Son, but gave him up for all of us, will he not with him also give us everything else?" (8:32). As we navigate through the peaks and valleys of our Christian journey, we ultimately find rest in the assurance that God loves us and will one day welcome us into his eternal presence. In this sense our sovereign God is working all things together for good for those who love him and are called according to his purposes. Some of his ways may remain a mystery to us, but we trust that "the one who began a good work among [us] will bring it to completion by the day of Jesus Christ" (Phil 1:6).

Discussion Questions

1. What are the main points of Romans 1–8? What is the reason for God's plan of salvation through Christ? What is the "mechanism" of this plan? How does this plan work in our lives?

2. Modern believers tend to apply Romans 7:24 to their current struggles with sin and temptation. I suggest that the "wretched person" of verse 24 is a Jewish person prior to his or her conversion. This person wants to obey the law but fails to do so because of sin. If Paul did write from a Jewish perspective here, is there any relevance for modern-day Christians in the text?

3. Can you recall a time when you turned to Romans 8:28 for encouragement and the situation did not seem to work out "for good"? How did that make you feel? Did you doubt God or your faith? What view of God underlies Paul's declaration that "all things work together for good for those who love God"? How could this understanding of God affect your reaction to the difficulties of life?

4. In day-to-day life, what are some things that make you aware of the fact that you are living between the "already" and the "not yet"? How do you live between these two poles? Where are the points of encouragement and discouragement?

For Further Reading

Charles B. Cousar, *A Theology of the Cross: The Death of Jesus in the Pauline Letters* (Minneapolis: Fortress, 1990).

Leander E. Keck, *Romans* (Abingdon New Testament Commentaries; Nashville: Abingdon, 2005).

Craig S. Keener, *Romans* (New Covenant Commentary Series; Eugene: Cascade, 2009).

Douglas J. Moo, *The Epistle to the Romans* (New International Commentary on the New Testament; Grand Rapids: Eerdmans, 1996).

Keith F. Nickle, "Romans 7:7-25," *Interpretation* 33 (1979): 181–87.

Chapter 5

Partaking of the Lord's Supper in an Unworthy Manner

1 Corinthians 11:27

When I was a child, our Lutheran church in Hong Kong celebrated the Lord's Supper every first Sunday of the month. One of the perks of getting past confirmation at the age of thirteen was the privilege of participating in Holy Communion. The wafer tasted rather flat, but the tiny plastic cup certainly did not contain Welch's grape juice! I felt so much like an adult, kneeling in front of the altar sipping real wine and praying for forgiveness of my adolescent transgressions. The sensation was a curious mix of solemnity and nervousness. On the one hand, I realized the seriousness of the sacraments, taking care not to drop the wafer or spill the wine. On the other hand, a nagging feeling of uneasiness dampened my gratitude for the body and blood of Jesus.

In searching for the root of that feeling, my thoughts bring me back to the passage my pastor recited at every Holy Communion:

> For I received from the Lord what I also handed on to you, that the Lord Jesus on the night when he was betrayed took a loaf of bread, and when he had given thanks, he broke it and said, "This is my body that is for you. Do this in remembrance of me." In the same way he took the cup also, after supper, saying, "This cup is the new covenant in my blood. Do this, as often as you drink it, in remembrance of me." For as often as you eat this bread and drink the cup, you proclaim the Lord's death until he comes. (1 Cor 11:23-26)

One might have expected the reading to end there, but he continued:

> Whoever, therefore, eats the bread or drinks the cup of the Lord in an unworthy manner will be answerable for the body and blood of the Lord. Examine yourselves, and only then eat of the bread and drink of the cup. For all who eat and drink without discerning the body, eat and drink judgment against themselves. (1 Cor 11:27-29)

It was not the words of Jesus, but the warnings of Paul, that frightened me. Regardless of what I had done that week, I did not want to be answerable for the body and blood of the Lord or to eat and drink judgment against myself. During the few minutes at the altar, I thought about my latest sins in order to squeeze in some self-examination before it was my turn to receive the elements. Even though verse 30, "For this reason many of you are weak and ill, and some have died," generally was not read at Communion, it made me feel even more anxious. Thanks to years of Sunday school, images of those on whom the wrath of God fell came swiftly to mind: Ananias and Sapphira dropped dead in front of Peter for lying to the Holy Spirit (Acts 5:1-11), the ground opened up and swallowed Korah and his company because they rebelled against Moses and Aaron (Num 16:31-35), and Uzzah was struck down by God when he tried to save the ark of the covenant from falling off a cart (2 Sam 6:6-7). Would it be better not to approach the Lord's Table at all if I did not confess every one of my sins beforehand? According to my thirteen-year-old reasoning, it was not worth the risk if the consequence was judgment—or even death.

Misinterpretations are often subtle and not always obvious. Sometimes people take a scriptural passage out of context to support a valid theological point. Regarding my young thoughts before the Lord's Table, doesn't the Bible teach us to confess our sins and keep short accounts with God? Aren't we assured that God is faithful and will forgive our sins, for he despises neither a broken spirit nor a contrite heart (1 John 1:9; Ps 51:17)? Yet the fear of damnation I got in my adolescent reading of Paul seems to contradict the invitational spirit of the Lord's Table. Communion is, after all, a way to remember Jesus' acceptance of sinners who became believers. Didn't Jesus share table with tax collectors and sinners (Mark 2:15-17; Luke 7:34)? Weren't his disciples arguing over who was the greatest even on the occasion of the first Lord's Supper (Luke 22:24-27)? If all the members of the Corinthian church had to be pure and blameless before receiving the Lord's Supper, there probably would not be a Lord's Supper of which to speak. The same could be said for us in our churches today. How unfortunate it would be if Christians considered themselves too unholy and unworthy to partake of the bread and cup with a clear conscience because of a misreading of this text.

In order for us to appreciate Paul's warning without allowing it to detract from our participation in Communion, we need to consider the back story. What lies behind these strong words within the context of the situation at Corinth? Given that Paul's letters are usually pastoral and situational, addressing specific problems in the life of his congregations, this discussion of the Lord's Supper is no exception. In fact, the segment quoted above, 1 Corinthians 11:23-29, is an excerpt from a larger literary unit that begins at verse 17 and ends at verse 34. Let us consider how the members of the Corinthian church might have understood Paul's exhortation when the letter was first read to them.

Wealth and Status: the Driving Forces of Corinth

Had Corinth not been a highly stratified, status-conscious society with a large gap between the rich and the poor, the celebration of the Lord's Supper at the Corinthian church might not have harmed Christian unity and equity. Paul's disapproval of the congregation is not because they have neglected to observe the sacrament, but because they have done it in a way that ignores the self-sacrifice embodied by Jesus. Therefore, unless they correct their understanding and practice of the Lord's Supper, it will be as though they never commemorated Christ's death at all.

Before we criticize the members of the Corinthian church for making a mockery of the Lord's Supper, we need to consider a few points. Many in this church were Gentiles by birth, steeped in the cultural conventions of the Greco-Roman world. Perhaps in learning to operate within the Christian community, some members of the church imported secular practices. In order to understand how they have become oblivious to their inappropriate approach to the Lord's Supper, we will examine the flavor of the city itself.

By the middle of the first century, Corinth had developed a reputation because of its geographic advantage, political stature, and economic savvy. Situated on an isthmus connecting the northern and southern regions of Greece, Corinth was flanked by two harbors. Goods were unloaded from a ship at one port, carried over land for a short distance, reloaded onto another ship at the second port, and then sent on their way. The transit through Corinth not only saved time, but also reduced the risk of seafaring disasters such as storms and the attacks of pirates. Julius Caesar must have recognized the potential of this location. After his Roman predecessors turned the Greek city into rubble in a defeat, Caesar rebuilt Corinth. The new Corinth was named the capital city of Achaia and shortly developed into a Roman colony. The Isthmian games and gladiatorial contests attracted tourists, the roads and port facilities attracted merchants, and the temples and shrines attracted religious adherents. Together with an already renowned bronze industry, Corinth blossomed into one of the main banking centers in Greece. The Corinthians were proud of themselves and their city's achievements, and some scaled the socioeconomic ladder quickly in a short time. As a result, the gulf between rich and poor widened, and the social hierarchies within the city became more and more defined.

To some extent, the church in Corinth depicted in Paul's letters seems to represent a microcosm of the city. In the segment on the Lord's Supper (11:17-34), the issue is not so much the multiethnic background but the socioeconomic differences between the members. Earlier in the letter, Paul addresses the problem of factions and reminds them that "not many of [them] were wise by human standards, not many were powerful, not many were of noble birth" (1:26); he points to their humble beginnings. We can infer that some, presumably not all, have since experienced upward mobility. In fact, with some sarcasm, Paul describes the current status of his opponents in the congregation: "We are fools for the sake of Christ, but you are wise in Christ. We are weak, but you are strong. You are held in honor, but we in disrepute" (4:10). From being neither wise, powerful, nor of noble birth, some members have become—at least in their own estimation—wise, strong, and honorable. We do not have enough information to pinpoint the identity of these troublemakers. Are they the same people who are stirring up the other various problems addressed in the letter? We don't know. However, even if these wealthy Christians represent a minority, they seem to have sufficient influence as an opposing force for Paul.

The tension between the rich and the poor comes to the foreground when the Corinthian house churches gather together to observe the Lord's Supper. Paul has learned how they celebrate it, and he finds their methods problematic. "When you come together," he writes, "it is not for the better but for the worse. . . . it is not really to eat the Lord's Supper" (11:17, 20). Knowing the Corinthian Christians' tendency toward conflict and the threat it poses to the unity of the church, Paul treats this problem with seriousness. He is even ready to challenge the genuineness of those who call themselves believers, since in their administering of the Lord's Supper they have brought about divisions within the church (11:18-19).

The Lord's Supper, Corinthian Style

Let's remember that we are making educated guesses about the situation at the Corinthians' Lord's Supper. The few details given by Paul, archaeological information on the size and layout of large homes of that period and locale, and our knowledge of ancient meal practices offer some help. Presumably, the number of Christians in Corinth is large enough that they have to meet in separate homes. Periodically, members from several house churches gather at the home of a wealthy patron for the Lord's Supper. Excavations of Roman villas near Corinth indicate that the main dining room, the *triclinium*, can accommodate nine to twelve guests comfortably reclined around a table. The overflow area, usually a nearby atrium, can seat another thirty or forty. By necessity, then, some members are invited to eat with the owner of the house in the plush surroundings of the *triclinium*, while the rest are relegated to the sparsely furnished courtyard.

Who gets to be on the short list of honorable guests? In a society where a person's social status is determined by birth and public acclaim, the host naturally saves the best places for his close friends and associates, people who by proximity will enhance his "honor quotient" among his peers. This practice is part of the symbolic significance of meals as a means of expressing friendship, solidarity, and unity. Following social decorum, the elite will eat with the elite. Since the poor and other lesser guests are in the house only because they come for the Lord's Supper, they are not considered honored guests in the true sense of the word. They may as well eat in the courtyard. We, like Paul, may not like such divisiveness within the family of God. However, this demonstration of the values of honor and shame that governed social protocol in the ancient Mediterranean world is neither surprising nor culturally inappropriate. In fact, a company of mixed socioeconomic status would have raised eyebrows. Even though Paul may argue for equal status when he writes later in the same letter, "For in the one Spirit we were all baptized into one body—Jews or Greeks, slaves or free—and we were all made to drink of one Spirit" (12:13; cf. Gal 3:28), in practice, social conditioning does not immediately disappear simply because people become Christians.

Not only is there disagreement over where people eat the Lord's Supper, but there is also disagreement regarding when they eat, how much they eat, and what they eat. Paul describes the practice at Corinth: "When the time comes to eat, each of you goes ahead with your own supper, and one goes hungry and another becomes drunk" (11:21). It is difficult to imagine someone getting drunk if we think about the tiny bit of bread or wafer and the sip of wine or juice that constitute our Holy Communion today. But when the sacramental rite is incorporated into the main meal, as is the case at Corinth, the breaking of the bread may occur before the supper, which is then followed by the blessing of the cup after the main meal. Another way is to finish the main meal first before holding a separate ceremony. Either way, there is time to eat and drink, and to drink excessively to the point of drunkenness.

The details of the scenario can be played out in several ways. One suggestion is that the inequity is a result of the patron's choice. In addition to opening up his home to stage the Lord's Supper, the wealthy member may choose to provide food for everyone in attendance. While his generosity bodes well for his social stature, it is not out of line for him to serve different grades of foods to different levels of guests. If there is a premium seating plan, why not a premium menu? Since covering the meal for all is expensive, a less generous host may limit his hospitality to the supply of bread and wine only. Another possibility is the BYOF ("bring your own food") arrangement minus the benefit of a potluck dinner. In other words, the wealthy member offers the space for the gathering, perhaps even designates who eats in the *triclinium* and who in the atrium, but each member is responsible for bringing his or her own supper. This scenario opens up the possibility that some of the poorest members have nothing to bring and end up going hungry (11:21-22).

Such a show of inequality in a Christian community is of course appalling. It seems that the Corinthian Lord's Supper goes even further: it lacks basic courtesy. When Paul complains, "Each of you goes ahead with your own supper" (11:21), the phrase "each of you" must refer to the most privileged folks at the supper. Otherwise, it does not make sense for everyone to be going ahead at the same time. If the formal celebration with bread and wine comes after the regular meal, the rich may have just gone ahead with their feast—whether brought from home or served by their wealthy patron—without bothering to wait for the poorer members whose late arrival after work may leave them with little or nothing to eat. Even if the Lord's Supper begins with the breaking of bread when all are present, the rich, if they are served first, still have an edge over the poor in the quantity and quality of food. For this reason, Paul tells the Corinthians to "wait for one another" (11:34). An alternate translation is to "receive one another," which calls for hospitality in both attitude and practice.

Even though the behavior of the elite at the Lord's Supper is understandable from a cultural perspective, it is reprehensible from a theological point of view. These wealthy Christians may have taken their cue from meals at trade associations to which they belong. But this is their blind spot: the church is not a guild or a club. Mutuality and justice must prevail over competitive one-upmanship. At Corinth, elevating the status of the rich comes at the cost of humiliating the poor and showing contempt for the church (11:22). This situation is a far cry from the ideal of the first Christians depicted in Acts: "All who believed were together and had all things in common; they would sell their possessions and goods and distribute the proceeds to all, as any had need" (Acts 2:44-47; 4:32-35). No wonder Paul is indignant. Repeatedly he voices his disapproval, "I do not commend you" (11:17, 22).

In order to override the Corinthians' pattern, Paul starts with Jesus, the Lord in whose honor the supper is held. It is not that the church has neglected to gather for the Lord's Supper; Paul commends them for maintaining the traditions he handed on to them (11:2). The problem is the manner in which they carry out the tradition. Not every member is at fault—only the elitist members who think they are gathering for the Lord's Supper while not caring when others around them go hungry. Has the sacramental meal turned into some kind of Greco-Roman dinner party that ignores the spirit with which Jesus established the Lord's Supper? If so, then the powerful minority needs a refresher course on the true intention of Communion. Paul seeks to change their attitude and actions for the common good.

From the Last Supper to the Lord's Supper

Paul's version of Jesus' words at the Last Supper is similar to that found in Luke 22:19-20, attesting to the faithful transmission of Jesus' teachings in the early church. The repetition of the command, "Do this in remembrance of me," in First Corinthians 11:24-25 may point to a set rendition that circulated by that time. Paul is not introducing anything new to the Corinthian Christians. From the start, he reminds them that Jesus originated the Eucharistic feast. The somber occasion of the Last Supper, "the night when he was betrayed" (11:23), stands in sharp contrast with the drunken revelry that sometimes occurs at the Corinthians' Lord's Supper (11:21). Even the words are to be recited seriously. The terms Paul uses, "I received . . . I also handed on," echo the technical language of rabbinic circles and Greco-Roman philosophical schools that showed the faithful transmission of the words of important teachers.

The backdrop of the Last Supper is the Jewish Passover. The Passover commemorates the fateful night when God's angels passed over the homes of the Israelites during the slaughtering of Egypt's firstborn (Exod 12:1-51). In Israel's history, the exodus is the definitive saving event of God's deliverance of his people. If God saved in the past, he will save again. Isaiah even describes God's promised salvation as a new exodus: "I am about to do a new thing; now it springs forth, do you not perceive it? I will make a way in the wilderness and rivers in the desert" (Isa 43:19). Therefore, by the time of Jesus, not only is Passover viewed as a feast of remembrance, but it also signifies the hope of God's future redemption in the coming of the Messiah. Since the celebration includes the offering of sacrifices, the atonement of the sin of God's people becomes part of the meaning of the Passover as well. Yahweh is a faithful God who keeps his covenant with his people. Deliverance and forgiveness of sins represent God's mercy in action.

The symbolic meanings behind the Passover—covenant, forgiveness, and redemption—are evident in Jesus' breaking of the bread and passing of the cup. "This is my body that is for you" (11:24). Some ancient manuscripts read "that is *broken* for you," whereas Luke has "given for you." The stress lies in the self-giving meaning of the Greek preposition *hyper*—for the sake of, or on behalf of, others. The same preposition is found in Jewish literature to speak of the way a martyr dies for God's law or for the sake of nobility, goodness, and virtue. Later in the same letter, Paul uses a similar construction: "Christ died for (*hyper*) our sins in accordance with the Scriptures" (15:3), as he also does in his letter to the Romans: "Christ died for (*hyper*) the ungodly. . . . Christ died for (*hyper*) us" (Rom 5:6, 8). The sense of Jesus' self-giving as a substitution recalls the function of the sacrificial animal, which made atonement for the sins of the worshiper possible. This idea is picked up in the book of Hebrews in which the author describes Jesus as appearing "once for all at the end of the age to remove sin by the sacrifice of himself" (Heb 9:26). In short, the emphasis is not on the brokenness of Jesus' body, even though the loaf is broken to be shared by all around the table, but on the fact that Jesus' death was other-centered. He died for the sake of others.

The meaning of the cup further explains the benefit of this death: "This cup is the new covenant in my blood" (11:25). The notion of a new covenant takes us back to the renewal promised by God through the prophet Jeremiah: "I will make a new covenant with the house of Israel and the house of Judah. . . . I will put my law within them, and I will write it on their hearts; and I will be their God, and they shall be my people. . . . for I will forgive their iniquity, and remember their sin no more" (Jer 31:31-34). While blood is not mentioned in Jeremiah, it brings to mind the ceremony in Exodus 24 that confirms the covenant between God and Israel. There Moses sprinkles the blood on the people and says, "See the blood of the covenant that the LORD has made with you in accordance with all these words" (Exod 24:8). Although the Israelites have maintained a dismal record in fulfilling their part of the covenant, the old covenant is still the foundation for the new. Jesus' blood now seals the new covenant, binding God to his promise not only to forgive his people but to empower them to live in faithful obedience to him.

Just as the Passover signifies Israel's gratitude for past deliverance and the hope for future salvation, Paul's interpretation of the Lord's Supper also points in both directions: "For as often as you eat this bread and drink the cup, you proclaim the Lord's death until he comes" (11:26). Christians stand between Jesus' Last Supper and his eventual Messianic Banquet. They stand between the assurance of salvation on account of Jesus' death and the guarantee of the final completion in the second coming of Jesus. In the meantime, until he comes, the Lord's Supper proclaims the self-giving nature and saving power of Jesus' death—verbally in the words of institution, and practically in the way in which believers relate to one another and to the world. As such, authentic remembrance never leaves one's life unaffected.

In partaking of the Lord's Supper together, believers affirm the vertical and horizontal dimensions of what it means to be the covenantal people of God. On the one hand, God reconciles the Corinthian Christians to himself through the death of Christ (2 Cor 5:19). On the other hand, this restored relationship should impact the way they treat one another. Here is where the wealthy members of the Corinthian congregation have veered off course. Jesus' death is "for you (*hyper hymōn*)"—for those in the main dining room as well as those in the overflow room—without distinction. The plurality in the pronoun *hymōn* ("you all" or "you people") is specific in the Greek but lost in the English translation. Similarly, the twice repeated command to "do this in remembrance of me" begins with a plural imperative (11:24-25), referring to everyone present in the wealthy patron's house. If the followers of Jesus are to imitate the Lord's example of humility and self-giving, why are the rich eating earlier, eating better food, eating more food, and eating more comfortably? How does this reflect the spirit with which Jesus instituted the Lord's Supper at his Last Supper? The difference is so pronounced that Paul is at a loss for words: "What should I say to you? Should I commend you? In this matter I do not commend you!" (11:22).

Warning and Remedy

Given the contrast between the significance Jesus placed on his meal of remembrance and the practice it has become among the Corinthian Christians, Paul's warnings in verses 27 to 34 highlight the gravity of the offense. Because the Lord's Supper is linked to Jesus' death, abusing the Lord's Supper is like rejecting the benefits of his death. Fortunately, these Christians have not set out to reject the saving gift of God. If they had, they would not have been a part of the Corinthian church and celebrated the Lord's Supper in the first place. It is true that they have approached the Lord's Supper "in an unworthy manner" (11:27), but they are not deemed unworthy—by Jesus or by Paul—to eat the bread and drink the cup.

What, then, is this "unworthy manner"? This is explained a few verses later by an equally mysterious phrase, "without discerning the body" (11:29). Whose body or what body is in view here? The Greek verb, *diakrinō*, almost always "discern" in most English translations, carries the sense of evaluating, recognizing, and judging. While an exact translation is difficult, the idea of taking something into careful consideration and acting accordingly seems to be in order. The challenge is to identify what "the body" refers to. I see two options.

First, perhaps "discerning the body" means reflecting thoughtfully on the body of Jesus, for the elements signify his sacrificial death and its resulting benefits. Arguing from the immediate context, the two other occurrences of the word "body" (*sōma* in Greek) in 11:17-34 clearly point to Jesus' body: "this is my body (*sōma*) that is for you" (11:24), and "answerable for the body (*sōma*) and blood of the Lord" (11:27). While it would be nice if Paul wrote "discerning the body (*sōma*) *and blood of the Lord*," the simpler "discerning the body" is meant to include both body and blood.

Second, "body" may refer to Christ's body as a metaphor for the church. In this reading the cue is taken from chapter 12, where Paul develops the theme of diversity and unity in the church: "For just as the body is one and has many members, and all the members of the body, though many, are one body, so it is with Christ" (12:12). The failure to discern the body, then, refers to the factions and divisiveness among the Corinthians. These may be caused by allegiance toward different human leaders (1:10-13), divisions along socioeconomic lines, or other factors.

Perhaps it is not necessary to choose one interpretation over the other. Paul's wording may be deliberately unclear, since it requires both interpretations of "discerning the body" in order to address the vertical *and* horizontal dimensions of the Lord's Supper. In fact, Paul does something similar when discussing the difference between eating at the table of the Lord versus the table of demons in chapter 10. He writes, "The cup of blessing that we bless, is it not a sharing in the blood of Christ? The bread that we break, is it not a sharing in the body of Christ? Because there is one bread, we who are many are one body, for we all partake of the one bread" (10:16-17). Here in verse 16 Paul speaks of both bread and blood in a parallel construction to emphasize the close connection between the believers and Jesus as they commemorate his death. The sharing cuts both ways. While they receive life through Jesus' sacrificial death, they also promise to live as he did—for others and not for themselves. The importance of Christian solidarity is further pressed in the image of one body of believers sharing one loaf of bread in verse 17. Hence Christ's body takes on both meanings: it is the body given to death (10:16), and it is Christians as members of his body, whose various parts are different yet indispensable (10:17; 12:12-27).

Disrespect for the Lord's Supper, as in the situation at Corinth, makes a mockery of the spirit with which Jesus gave his body and blood. It destroys Christian unity. There is nothing loving when "one goes hungry and another becomes drunk" (11:21). Such contempt for a sacred ritual of remembrance will result in severe consequences. The perpetrators are placed in the company of those who are guilty of putting Jesus to death and "answerable for the body and blood of the Lord" (11:27). By showing contempt for the church, their own status as genuine believers becomes suspect. By humiliating those who have nothing, they humiliate the Lord they set out to honor (11:19, 22). Instead of eating and drinking to express gratitude for the gift of life, they "eat and drink judgment against themselves" (11:29). In Paul's opinion, their sins are already judged, given the illnesses and deaths among them (11:30).

God's present judgment on the Corinthian church is bearable compared to being "condemned along with the world" in the final accounting (11:31). While God disciplines those he loves (Heb 12:6, 10; Deut 8:5), the Corinthian Christians can still reform their ways and come to the Lord's table in a worthy manner. Even though Paul directs his warning and remedy mainly toward the rich members who mistreat others to boost their own status, Paul's words are instructive for the entire congregation. Even as he exhorts the rich to be considerate and hospitable to the poor, the unspoken expectation is for the poor to do likewise by letting bygones be bygones.

Following his fury, Paul brings the discussion to a close in a more friendly tone: "So then, my brothers and sisters, when you come together to eat, wait for one another" (11:33). Even though the elitist members have done the exact opposite of what it means to partake of the Lord's Supper, Paul takes for granted that the house churches will continue to observe this tradition *when*—not if—they come together. The Lord's Supper, however, must not be confused with a Greco-Roman dinner party. If eating at home ahead of time can solve the problem of discourtesy at the common meal, then the rich are welcome to do what it takes to avoid shaming the poor in public (11:34). Paul is practical in navigating these pastoral waters. He does not forbid the enjoyment of good food for those who can afford it, as long as the haves do not shame the have-nots by flaunting their abundance. But if status and social norms get in the way of Christian love and unity, then there can be no compromise. For the sake of unity, the rich can either give up their rights to have an extravagant dinner party while the poor look on, or they can share their resources with those who have less.

Conclusion

My childhood fear of taking the Lord's Supper in an unworthy manner as an offense punishable by death is unsound. I have studied Paul's recitation of the words of institution and the warnings in their historical and literary settings, and my experience of Holy Communion has been transformed. The mockery of the Lord's Supper at Corinth lies not in a disrespect of Jesus' death, but in the wealthy members' disregard of Jesus' self-giving spirit. Had they followed Jesus' example, they would not have given the disadvantaged members such shameful treatment as late food, bad food, and even no food. The vertical and horizontal dimensions of the Lord's Supper demand that each person be at peace with Jesus and his or her neighbor. The symbolic rite of the Lord's Supper is a regular reminder of the two greatest and inseparable commandments: "You shall love the Lord your God with all your heart, and with all your soul, and with all your mind," and "you shall love your neighbor as yourself" (Matt 22:37, 39). It is no longer only a matter between Jesus and the worshiper.

Within our Christian communities today, socioeconomic status is one of many causes of division. Political, ideological, and even theological differences hinder our communion with one another in the body of Christ.

Feeding our self-righteousness and pride, our "we-they" mentality needs reexamination too. Next time we celebrate the Lord's Supper, whether we go to the altar to receive the elements or pass the bread and cup along the pews, we do well to "discern the body" by being grateful for Jesus' sacrifice on our behalf and for the spiritual kinship of those around us. Let our fear at the Lord's Supper consist of awe and not of fright.

Discussion Questions

1. Think about the way your church or tradition celebrates the Lord's Supper. What is said? How do you receive the elements? How do you celebrate it? What helps you connect to Jesus and the spirit with which he instituted the Last Supper to his disciples?

2. Socioeconomic inequality, among other things, threatened the unity of the Corinthian church. Is there a threat to your church's unity? Are there ways to address the problem before it does great damage?

3. When the Corinthian congregation came together for the Lord's Supper, the elites excluded people from their rich meal. For them, cultural norms became an excuse for thoughtlessness and unfairness. Do you see this kind of thing happening at your church? Is it obvious, or is it subtle?

4. In what way is Paul's exhortation to the Corinthians in the matter of the Lord's Supper a test case for the principle, "All things are lawful, but not all things are beneficial" (1 Cor 10:23)?

For Further Reading

Mark P. Surburg, "The Situation at the Corinthian Lord's Supper in Light of 1 Corinthians 11:21: A Reconsideration," *Concordia Journal* 32 (2006): 17–37.

Gerd Theissen, "Social Integration and Sacramental Activity: An Analysis of 1 Cor. 11:17-34," in *The Social Setting of Pauline Christianity: Essays on Corinth*, ed. and trans. John H. Schütz (Philadelphia: Fortress: 1982) 145–74.

Anthony C. Thiselton, *The First Epistle to the Corinthians: A Commentary on the Greek Text* (Grand Rapids: Eerdmans, 2000).

Ben Witherington III, *Conflict and Community in Corinth: A Socio-Rhetorical Commentary on 1 and 2 Corinthians* (Grand Rapids: Eerdmans, 1995).

Chapter 6

Speaking the Truth in Love

Ephesians 4:15

"I couldn't get myself to tell her. I was afraid it would hurt her feelings."

"But you must! Don't you know the Bible tells us to speak the truth in love?"

"I know, but what if she is not ready to hear the truth?"

"You'll just have to figure out a way to say it. It's for her own good."

It is not difficult to imagine a conversation like this taking place. Something needs to be said, but the blunt truth may be difficult for the other person to hear. The speaker struggles to find the right words. In the end, she may do as Paul exhorts the Ephesian congregation to do: "speak the truth in love." Many modern readers assume this is the sense of Ephesians 4:15—to tell someone something, even if it may cause hurt feelings, when it's for the person's own good.

A quick online search for the phrase "speaking the truth in love" yields references from articles and blog entries on Christian websites. In the majority of the cases, the phrase denotes some form of truth-telling. Below are typical examples:

Speaking the truth in love is: Truth (reproof and/or warning) communicated with affirmation and encouragement, and firmly established on a historical relationship of caring and commitment.[1]

In institutional affairs, as well as in affairs of the heart, we do well to "speak the truth, in love." . . . Leaders of all kinds of institutions tend to think that fudging the truth from time to time will keep the institution stable and whole; they tend to believe that transparency is just threatening.[2]

We speak the truth in love—with a view to saving souls. We speak the truth to uplift and comfort the fainthearted. We speak the truth to restore those who have wandered from God and into sin. We speak the truth to instruct and exhort. We speak the truth to encourage and admonish. We speak the truth to correct and persuade. Always, always, we speak the truth to glorify God.[3]

Whether the context is communication, integrity, evangelism, or discipleship, the idea of speaking the truth in love is taken by these writers to mean not to lie, mislead, or conceal the truth. In the third example, the phrase "speak the truth in love" is even shortened to "speak the truth." The content of "the truth," presumably, is whatever is appropriate to the situation at hand.

Telling the truth out of a loving motive is of course Christian and biblical. The question is not whether Paul exhorts the believers to treat one another with honesty, but whether this is what Paul means in Ephesians when he writes, "But speaking the truth in love, we must grow up in every way into him who is the head, into Christ, from whom the whole body, joined and knit together by every ligament with which it is equipped, as each part is working properly, promotes the body's growth in building itself up in love" (4:15-16). That Ephesians 4:15 is easily taken out of context may have to do with its proximity to a different verse in the same chapter: "So then, putting away falsehood, let all of us speak the truth to our neighbors, for we are members of one another" (4:25). Verses 15 and 25 are sometimes taken to mean the same thing and used interchangeably, as shown in the following example found in the Bible study material of a popular Christian magazine:

But a faithful friend must sometimes speak words that bring pain. If your words hurt, are they spoken lovingly? And are they offered as "faithful wounds," the kind that are necessary for your friend's best interests? Speaking the truth can be done without love—even with a friend. But "speaking the truth in love" means you speak with respect, gentleness, and kindness—maintaining your friend's dignity. (See also Job 42:7-9; Ephesians 4:25–5:2; James 1:5-8.)[4]

Note the way in which the wording of one verse is used while the reference of the other is given. Had the author quoted "speaking the truth to our neighbors" instead of "speaking the truth in love," the inconsistency would at least have been less. After all, in Ephesians 4:25, "putting away falsehood" is the way to carry out Paul's appeal, "let us all speak the truth to our neighbors." In fact, Paul has borrowed that phrase from the prophet Zechariah: "Speak truth everyone with his neighbor; judge truth and peaceable judgment in your gates" (Zech 8:16). Paul's wording in Ephesians 4:25 (*laleite alētheian hekastos meta tou plēsion auto*) is almost identical, word for word, to that of Zechariah in the Septuagint, the Greek translation of the Hebrew Scriptures (*laleite alētheian hekastos pros ton plēsion autou*), except for a slight alteration from "with his neighbor" to "to our neighbor." In Zechariah, the context promotes bearing honest testimonies before judges and magistrates, whereas Paul's instruction leaves room for a broader application of truth-telling.

I propose that, in the context of Ephesians 4, "speaking the truth in love" has a narrower application. The phrase refers to proclaiming the pure gospel (as described in the first three chapters of Ephesians) in order to counter the false teachings that threaten the unity of the church. It does not refer to any or all truths, but to the authentic presentation of God's plan of salvation. To arrive at this interpretation, we must consider both the immediate context of the phrase in Ephesians 4:1-16 and also the broader context of the whole letter.

Ephesians: an Overview

Compared to Paul's letters to the Corinthian and Galatian churches, in which he responds to specific problems in those congregations, the letter to the Ephesians deals with more general issues. This leads scholars to think it could have circulated among multiple congregations in Asia Minor. Matters concerning God's salvation, church unity, interpersonal ethics, and household codes were relevant in all those churches.

The letter is neatly divided into two halves. In the first three chapters, Paul presents God's plan of salvation and its grounding in God's divine love and power. In the last three chapters, he discusses what it means to live as God's children and members of God's household.

In Ephesians 1–3, God's plan of salvation is framed in Paul's familiar grouping of faith, hope, and love. Out of God's divine love and grace, he chooses to gather up all things in heaven and on earth to himself. By the blood of Jesus, forgiveness of sins is granted to those who through faith receive this offer of redemption. No longer destined for destruction, believers are raised with Jesus and become God's children of light. At the present, they are sealed with the Holy Spirit, who is God's guarantee of their hope of future inheritance.

The theme of God's mystery is underscored in these opening chapters. Playing off the secrecy of pagan mystery cults, Paul declares that God's mystery, hidden until now, is fully revealed through the work of Jesus Christ. Specifically, the mystery involves breaking down the wall of hostility between Jews and Gentiles by Jesus, who brings peace between them. Formerly enemies, Jewish and Gentile believers are now part of a new humanity. Since in Christ they are all God's children and fellow heirs of God's promises, Paul describes them as members of the same body.

While this mystery may seem obvious to us modern Christians—it's the path of God's plan of salvation from the Old Testament to the New—we can at least imagine that it must have been unexpected for the peoples of the ancient Mediterranean world. The Jews had always understood themselves to be the chosen people of God. To them, the Gentiles represented everything unclean in the eyes of a holy God and his holy people. Likewise, the Gentile world viewed the Jews with suspicion. A people who worshiped only one God, refused to work on a particular day of the week, and separated themselves from the rest of society did not endear themselves to the pagans. Even with the work of Jesus, the movement from hatred to peace might still encounter challenges. Anticipating these difficulties, Paul addresses in the latter half of his letter what it means for believers of diverse backgrounds to demonstrate Christian unity in their lives together.

Briefly, Ephesians 4–6 contains exhortations for believers to live in a manner worthy of their Christian calling. To counter the temptation to revert to old ways of being, Paul urges the Ephesian Christians to operate out of a Spirit-filled life and a renewed mindset. Structures of society are to be grounded in a new Christian ethic. While hierarchical relationships between husband and wife, parent and child, and master and slave do not become void simply because a person becomes a Christian, a new emphasis on mutual love and respect will characterize all human interactions within the community of faith. Since unity and love reflect God's oneness, these qualities ought to characterize God's children. Moreover, unity behind the sound proclamation of the gospel is crucial if the church wants to wage a successful war against earthly authorities and spiritual powers of evil that threaten God's kingdom.

To have integrity as God's redeemed people, then, the church must live as one united people of God. Paul drives home this point in the first sixteen verses of chapter 4, where he holds the diversity and the unity of the church in positive tension. The primary image is that of the church as a body with Jesus Christ as its head. In the remainder of this chapter, we will look at

Ephesians 4:1-16 closely. We will set our phrase of interest, "speaking the truth in love" (4:15), in proper context.

Christian Unity: Rationale and Attitude

The first six verses of chapter 4 function as an introduction to the discussion of church unity and set the tone for the second half of the letter. Paul begins by entreating his readers to "lead a life worthy of the calling to which [they] have been called" (4:1). The repetition of "calling" and "called" is not a redundancy. These words remind the readers that they are the recipients of divine initiative. Being called by God is a privilege that comes with responsibility. Once called, the way in which they conduct themselves must be worthy of their newfound identity in Christ. In short, they must now live up to who they are.

Having received "the seal of the promised Holy Spirit" (1:13) and embraced Jesus who "proclaimed peace to [those] who were far off and peace to those who were near" (2:17), the Gentile and Jewish believers of Ephesus are urged to "[make] every effort to maintain the unity of the Spirit in the bond of peace" (4:3). Even though these Christians cannot take credit for creating the unity between them and their former enemies, they have the responsibility to protect it. Yet Paul is mindful that this new unity is fragile and in need of strengthening. So when he tells the Ephesians to "[make] every effort," he uses the Greek verb *spoudazō*, which connotes urgency as well as the process of working hard to keep peace and unity.

To strengthen the bond of peace, Paul suggests three other-centered relational attitudes (4:2). First is humility (*tapeinophrosunē*). Although in secular Greek this word implies servility, in the New Testament it is used for the praiseworthy attitude of submissiveness, when a person places other people's needs and interests over his or her own (Phil 2:3; Col 3:12; 1 Pet 5:5). In this regard, the greatest example is Christ, who "humbled (*etapeinōsen*) himself and became obedient to the point of death—even death on a cross" (Phil 2:8). "Humility" (*tapeinophrosunē*) and "humbled" (*etapeinōsen*) share the same root word. By his self-giving death, Christ models the humility with which his followers ought to relate to one another.

Second, hand in hand with the attitude of humility is that of gentleness (*prautētos*). These two qualities are the same ones Jesus uses to describe himself: "I am gentle (*praus*) and humble (*tapeinos*) in heart" (Matt 11:29). Gentleness or meekness requires that one does not insist on his or her rights, but puts aside self-interest for the sake of the common good.

Third, patience (*makrothumias*) is needed when humility and gentleness do not yield their desired result in a timely manner. In the Old Testament, God refers to himself as "slow to anger (*makrothumos*) and abounding in steadfast love" (Exod 34:6; see also Ps 86:15; Isa 57:15). In light of God's patience for his wayward people, is it too much to ask the Ephesian Christians to show patience and compassion for one another? Just as Jesus teaches his disciples to "be merciful as your Father is merciful" (Luke 6:36), the same could be said of divine imitation here: "Be patient as your Father is patient."

The final clause, "bearing (*anechomenoi*) with one another in love," reiterates the need for patience. The Greek verb *anechomai* implies endurance. Unity is meaningless and impossible unless it is sustained "in love," a note sounded both in the beginning and at the end of this section (4:2, 16). Love is the foundational commitment. Without it, the Christian community cannot stand. Yet this is not merely a love that individual members can provide out of selflessness or compassion. According to Paul, the love of the Christian community has as its source and power the very love of God himself. "In love," God chooses to bestow his blessings on believers (1:4). In spite of being dead in their trespasses (2:1-6), they are made alive with Christ out of God's great love. Because of God's mercy and divine initiative, Paul can pray for his congregation that "Christ may dwell in [their] hearts through faith, as [they] are being rooted and grounded in love" (3:17). In effect, the love shown by Christians is ideally a reflection of their true understanding of God's love for them in the first place.

To recap, it takes humility, gentleness, and patience to bear with one another in love. If practiced consistently, they will gradually become part of the ethos of the community, setting in motion a virtuous cycle moving believers from mutual tolerance to genuine love and concern for one another.

Besides, Christian unity makes theological sense because it is founded on the oneness that characterizes God. Upon exhorting his readers to "maintain the unity of the Spirit in the bond of peace" (4:3), Paul launches into a sevenfold declaration that links the oneness of believers to that of the Father, Son, and Spirit: "There is one body and one Spirit, just as you were called to the one hope of your calling, one Lord, one faith, one baptism, one God and Father of all, who is above all and through all and in all" (4:4-6). It is possible that this litany is drawn from ancient Christian liturgy (cf. 1 Cor 8:6; 12:12-13). The list begins with "one body," the key image for the church throughout the letter (1:23; 2:16-18; 4:12, 16; 5:23, 30). Paul insists that the Ephesian church is to operate as one body, with its members joined together and mutually dependent on one another. The oneness of shared Christian experience—one hope of eternal salvation, one response of faith, and one public witness of Christian baptism—is intertwined with the oneness of the three persons of the triune God—one Spirit, one Lord, and one God and Father of all. In short, the believers of the Ephesian church, regardless of their starting points (whether Jew or Gentile), have no reason to display anything other than unity if they take their calling seriously and live according to its expectations. To achieve this ideal as followers of Christ, they are not without resources. The one God and Father whom they worship is "above all and through all and in all" (4:6). His sovereign power and presence will ensure that the believers will receive what is needed for the whole body of Christ to grow in unity and in love.

The Church as the Body of Christ

In chapter 1, Paul introduces the metaphor of the body to refer to the church, with Christ as its head: "And [God] has put all things under [Christ's] feet and has made him the head over all things for the church, which is his body, the fullness of him who fills all in all" (1:22-23). When the resurrected Jesus is enthroned above the heavens, God grants him authority over the entire universe. Note, however, that Paul describes Jesus as the "head over all things *for* the church." Even though Jesus has power over everything, the church is, in fact, the main beneficiary of his headship. Later in the letter Paul refers to Jesus as the "head *of* the church" (5:23; cf. 4:15). Not only does Jesus have authority over the church, but he is also its source of life and power.

Jesus exercises his headship over the church by "filling" the church. As God the Father is "above all and through all and in all" (4:6), the risen Christ is the one "who fills all [and is] in all" (1:23). God fills Jesus in order for Jesus to fill his church with all his divine fullness. Although this language of "filling" and "fullness" is not specific, it captures a sense of grandeur and richness. Believers are endowed with the grace, gifts, and presence of God, mediated through Christ, their head, because they are his body. This is why it is important to be united: there is only one Christ, and Christ is the head of only one body.

A sharp observer may notice that the image of the body of Christ in Ephesians is slightly different from that of 1 Corinthians 12:12-27. In 1 Corinthians, the particular parts of the body—the foot, the hand, the ear, and the eye—are represented with equal value. The foot and the hand are as much parts of the whole body as the ear and the eye, even though the ear and the eye belong to a person's head and not his or her body. In Ephesians, the identification of Christ as the head sets him apart from the rest of the body, and specific body parts are not named. It seems that Paul's emphasis here is not on the equal status and treatment of different members, but on the authority of Christ over his church. Christ's headship highlights what he does for the body to direct its overall functioning and growth—something the body, if headless, cannot do for itself.

Paul is keenly aware that unity does not mean uniformity. In the next section (4:7-16), he discusses the array of spiritual gifts that Christ has given to the church to enhance its growth and effectiveness. Possessing gifts alone, however, is not enough. The growth of the body will not happen unless individual members cooperate with one another and exercise their gifts for the benefit of the whole. They must take advantage of their diversity in order to achieve unity. Because of its length, we will focus on this section in two parts: unity and diversity (4:7-11) and church growth and its related threats (4:12-16). We will address our focal phrase, "speaking the truth in love," in the second subsection.

Unity and Diversity, 4:7-11

Paul identifies two levels of gifts within the church—a general bestowal of gifts (4:7) and the gifts of specific church leaders (4:11). First, without spelling out exactly what the general forms of gifts to the church look like, Paul states that "*each of us* was given grace." This ensures that nobody is exempt from the charge to "[maintain] the unity of the Spirit in the bond of peace" (4:3). The democratization of grace entails the democratization of responsibility. Unity requires that each person fall in step with his or her fellow believers for the sake of the common good. Since these are gifts of grace, received with freedom and gratitude, there is no place for boasting of personal generosity or special achievement. If the gifts are not used for their intended purpose, it will be difficult to sustain peace, and the bond may be broken altogether.

Second, in verse 11 Paul lists various leaders within the church: "The gifts [Christ] gave were that *some* would be apostles, *some* prophets, *some* evangelists, *some* pastors and teachers" (4:11). This is by no means an exhaustive list, nor does it include everyone in the church. Presumably these offices are already in place in the Ephesian church, as no additional explanation is provided. In his first letter to the Corinthians, Paul also discusses spiritual gifts in their variety—the gifts of wisdom, knowledge, faith, healing, miracle-working, prophecy, discernment of spirits, tongues, interpretation of tongues. All these gifts originate from the same Spirit (1 Cor 12:4-11). In Ephesians the offices are likewise gifts of the one Lord to his church. Note that the list in Ephesians consists of people—apostles, evangelists, prophets, pastors, and teachers—not ministries. Perhaps this further underscores the fact that people, not functions, make or break the church.

Common to apostles, evangelists, prophets, pastors, and teachers is the responsibility of teaching the congregation. We will return shortly to the emphasis on proper teaching in the church of Ephesus, which is related to our understanding of what Paul means by "speaking the truth in love." At this point, we need to clarify the puzzling quotation and parenthetical statement of 4:8-10. It is sandwiched between the declaration of general and specific gifts of grace from the Lord.

The quotation in verse 8 is meant to support Paul's claim in verse 7 that Jesus Christ has the rightful authority to dispense his gift of grace to the church: "Therefore it is said, 'When he ascended on high he made captivity itself a captive; he gave gifts to his people'" (4:8). At first glance, this seems to be an odd choice of Old Testament Scripture for Paul to make a point. The problem is further complicated by the fact that the wording of Ephesians 4:8 is similar to but also different from two possible sources—either Psalm 68:18 from the Old Testament, or the rewording of Psalm 68:18 in the Targums, the Aramaic paraphrase of the Hebrew Scriptures. All three passages are shown below for comparison:

> When he ascended on high he made captivity itself a captive; he gave gifts to his people. (Eph 4:8)

> You ascended the high mount, leading captives on your train and receiving gifts from people. (Ps 68:18, Old Testament)

> You ascended the firmament, Prophet Moses; you took captivity captive; you learned the words of the law; you gave them as gifts to the sons of men. (Ps 68:18, Targums)

While Paul is not obligated to quote either of these sources exactly, is it possible to understand the logic of his strategy if he deliberately changed the wording to suit his purpose?

In the Old Testament, the general context of Psalm 68 involves the victory of God over his enemies. On his way up Mount Zion, God parades his captives in a triumphal procession. Since New Testament writers frequently give to Jesus the titles and functions of God himself in the Old Testament, it is understandable that Paul selects this psalm to reflect on Jesus Christ, whose death and resurrection result in his ascent into "the heavenly places, far above all rule and authority and power and dominion" (1:21; cf. 4:10). The most glaring alteration, however, from the psalm to Paul's wording is from God *receiving* gifts to Jesus *giving* gifts. In the Old Testament, the gifts God receives are tributes paid to him by his captives, but the gifts Jesus gives are spiritual gifts to equip the church. In other words, even if Paul uses Psalm 68:18 as a starting point, he has colored the Old Testament verse with a Jesus-centered reinterpretation.

The Targums are an Aramaic paraphrase of the Hebrew Scriptures, so they already reflect a rereading of Psalm 68:18. The scenario of the ascent of God to Mount Zion is reworked to describe the ascent of Moses to Mount Sinai to receive the law, which he in turn gives as a gift to Israel. If Paul began with the Targums, he would have retained the giving of the gifts and merely replaced Moses with Jesus. Is Paul underscoring the superiority of Jesus over Moses, the revered teacher for the Jews, since he will list teaching officers of the church a few verses later? This argument might seem plausible except that Moses factors nowhere near the context of Ephesians 4, or for that matter, of the letter as a whole. Introducing Moses here would seem awkward.

In short, Ephesians 4:8 fits neither Psalm 68:18 from the Old Testament nor the Targums of Psalm 68:18 perfectly. Presenting both possibilities allows us to weigh the strength of each argument, and in this case, Psalm 68:18 from the Old Testament seems to prevail. By applying to Jesus a psalm that praises God's victory, Paul affirms the supreme authority of the risen Christ. Jesus now endows his people, the church, with his bountiful gifts. As for Christ's captives, Paul has not made clear who they are. Maybe they are the evil powers and principalities conquered by Jesus' death and resurrection (cf. Col 2:15).

Perhaps Paul is aware that his use of Psalm 68:18 is not immediately obvious, so he gives a parenthetical statement in the next two verses to clarify the impact of Jesus' glorification: "When it says, 'He ascended,' what does it mean but that he had also descended into the lower parts of the earth? He who descended is the same one who ascended far above all the heavens, so that he might fill all things" (4:9-10). If "he ascended" refers to Jesus' exaltation in heaven, then "he had also descended" is best interpreted as Jesus' incarnation and work on the cross. This fits with the U-shaped course drawn by Paul in the famous Christ Hymn in Philippians of Christ's birth in human likeness and his exaltation by God after his death (Phil 2:6-11). Here again in Ephesians, Paul restates the point that the same Jesus who walked the face of the earth is the same Lord who now sits at the right hand of God in heaven (1:20). The suggestion that Jesus' descent "into the lower parts of the earth" refers to a trip to Hades is foreign to the context of this letter. Nowhere in Ephesians is there mention of Jesus going down to the underworld.

The key point in 4:7-11 is that Christ graciously gives general and specific gifts to the church. The insertion of verses 8-10 is Paul's argument (though complicated to us) that he indeed has the authority to do so. Even though unpacking verses 8-10 took some space in our discussion, it has allowed us to see the subtle connection with the saving work of Christ already described at length in Ephesians 1 and 2.

Church Growth and Its Threats, 4:12-16

The result of Christ's elevation is his privilege to fill all things—particularly his church—with his fullness. One expression of this divine fullness comes in the form of spiritual gifts to make the church grow. The direction of growth is expressed in the next two verses. Here we pick up the second half of the sentence following the listing of church leaders: ". . . to equip the saints for the work of ministry, for building up the body of Christ, until all of us come to the unity of the faith and of the knowledge of the Son of God, to maturity, to the measure of the full stature of Christ" (4:12-13). The reader can almost sense Paul's excitement as he piles phrase upon phrase to show a positive ongoing cycle of training within the community of faith. We already know Christ has given spiritual gifts to all members of the church, and to some he has assigned specific roles of leadership. These leaders are responsible for enabling other believers to develop their gifts, so that all may share in the work of ministry. Elsewhere Paul also instructs the Corinthian church to take advantage of the diversity of gifts among its congregants (1 Cor 14). In their case, the gifts of prophecy and tongues, when properly exercised, should build up the church and bear effective witness to nonbelievers. Any other form of personal showcasing in the name of "spirituality on display" is childish and disruptive to community life.

With every member contributing to the collective life of the church, the body of Christ is strengthened. In English, when we think of "bodybuilding," we think of Nautilus weight-training equipment at a gym. In the Greek, the image would actually be a physical structure, a literal building. Paul is reinforcing a metaphor that he has already introduced in chapter 2, where he speaks of the church as a holy temple "built (*epoikodomēthentes*) upon the foundation of the apostles and the prophets, with Christ Jesus himself as the cornerstone" (2:20). Hence "building up (*oikodomē*) the body of Christ" in 4:12 consists of two metaphors. The church is likened to Christ's body as well as Christ's temple. Each analogy is fitting. A body cannot live without its head any more than a temple can stand without its cornerstone. When the two images are used together, the overall effect is a connection between Christ and his church.

Is the building up of the church meant to be in quantity or quality? The ideal answer would be both, as a healthy church ought to grow in numbers as well as in spiritual depth. However, it does seem that Paul emphasizes in verse 12 the quality of the congregation. If there is quality, quantity will follow; but the reverse may not be true. The church, within the reality of its diversity, must move toward "unity of the faith and of the knowledge of the Son of God," "maturity," and "the full stature of Christ" (4:13). If this goal is kept at the forefront, a spiritually mature congregation will naturally draw people.

To unpack the elements of this goal further, verse 13 may be divided into two sets of criteria. First is "unity of the faith and of the knowledge of the Son of God." Both refer here not to the believers' faithfulness or their personal knowledge of Jesus, but to the objective content of salvation. In other words, a believer's faith is grounded in what the Son of God has done on his or her behalf. Amid the diversity in ethnicity, backgrounds, or spiritual gifts within the church, all members must stick to a singular confession—one hope, one Lord, one faith, and one baptism (4:4-5)—in order for the entire body to operate in peace and unity.

Second, "maturity" and "the full stature of Christ" are also related concepts. In the Greek, the phrase translated "to maturity" literally reads "to mature manhood." Here is the picture of a fully grown adult male, mature in physique and mind. The church, likened to a body with Christ as its head, is to emerge as a "mature corporate Christ." Of course the church does not become identical to Jesus Christ; that is not the point. The image here requires some imagination, for the historical Jesus is not in view. Rather, it recalls the notion of "one new man" (or "one new humanity") in Ephesians 2, referring to the unity created by Christ's work of reconciliation between Jewish and Gentile Christians (2:15). The maturity of this "one corporate Christ-body" will measure up to "the full stature of Christ," to the extent that Christ himself fills it. Put differently, the church will strengthen and mature as one united body in a way that is appropriate to its calling, identity, and equipping.

The maturity of the body of Christ takes time and is not without hazards, especially for a fledgling church in a pagan city. Paul identifies one pressing danger in particular that threatens to tear the church apart and warns his congregation: "We must no longer be children, tossed to and fro and blown about by every wind of doctrine, by people's trickery, by their craftiness in deceitful scheming" (4:14). False teachings may have already entered the church and begun to disrupt unity. Here and in the next chapter, Paul indicts the tricksters: "Let no one deceive you with empty words, for because of these things the wrath of God comes on those who are disobedient" (5:6). The exact nature of the heresies is unknown, though they were likely varied false teachings—"every wind of doctrine." Whatever they may be, these tainted "non-gospels" that seem to ring true but are not, whether they start within the church or come from the pagan world, are capable of disrupting "the unity of the faith" and distorting "the knowledge of the Son of God" within the church if left unchecked (4:13).

Paul exposes the evil of those sowing false teachings as if to say, "They are cheats, cheats, and, let me repeat, cheats!" Trickery, craftiness, and deceitful scheming all involve manipulation of the unwary, especially those still immature in their faith. In the pagan world, these words are used to describe dishonest players of dice who use weighted game pieces to fool others for personal gain. When this misrepresentation of the truth of the gospel circulates among believers, it attacks the church at its core.

Therefore, Paul insists that the Ephesian Christians must grow up and stand firm: "We must no longer be children, tossed to and fro and blown about by every wind of doctrine" (4:14). First, they must aim at becoming "the mature man" (4:13), as a child tends to be both foolish and easy to fool. The picture of a rudderless boat, tossed by the waves in the rough seas, is a disaster waiting to happen. It points to the indecision and instability among those who, like children, lack mature knowledge of their saving faith. Second, note the contrast between "man" in the singular and "children" in the plural. If each member represents a different child operating on his or her own, all these children are separately at risk of being deceived. They are easy targets. But as one united front, standing firm like a "mature man," the church is better prepared to fend off doctrinal attacks when its members agree on the truth of the gospel.

On the one hand, the church must guard against false teachings. On the other hand, those appointed as leaders must train and correct other members by "speaking the truth in love" (4:15a). In doing so, the pure teaching of the gospel will pervade the entire body of Christ. Instead of manipulation and trickery, the good news of salvation is to be offered in love. After all, it is in love that God has first purposed to pour out his blessings to those who believe (1:3-4).

The content of the good news of salvation offered in love is truth. Let us consider Paul's use of the term "truth" elsewhere in the same letter. In three other instances where the word appears, it refers to the gospel rather than to a general piece of information that is accurate and not fabricated. First, in describing the readers' conversion, Paul writes, "In [Christ] you also, when you had heard the word of truth, the gospel of your salvation, and had believed in him, were marked with the seal of the promised Holy Spirit" (1:13). "Truth" is identified as the good news in this verse. Second, when speaking of the Ephesians' conversion from an old self in paganism to a new self in Christ, Paul writes, "For surely you have heard about [Christ] and were taught in him, as truth is in Jesus" (4:21). Here, "truth" has to be passed on, taught by teachers, and learned by new converts. While "truth" refers also to the new code of conduct befitting of a follower of Jesus, all outward action is meaningless unless the gospel of salvation is correctly understood and embraced. Third, at the end of the epistle, Paul introduces the image of the whole armor of God that Christians must put on to engage in spiritual warfare against the powers of evil. The "belt of truth," the "breastplate of righteousness," the "shield of faith," and the "helmet of salvation" provide a protective covering for these Christian soldiers. They are equipped to proclaim "the gospel of peace," wielding the "sword of the Spirit, which is the word of God" (6:13-17). Again, the integrity of the gospel is at the forefront of Paul's mind. "Speaking the truth in love," then, has a specific referent: the phrase means proclaiming the truth of the gospel as empowered by God's love.

The remainder of the section expresses the commitment of the church to growth and unity. This is made possible as each member bears witness to the true gospel: "But speaking the truth in love, we must grow up in every way into him who is the head, into Christ, from whom the whole body, joined and knit together by every ligament with which it is equipped, as each part is working properly, promotes the body's growth in building itself up in love" (4:15-16). Once again the main image is that of the church as a body with Christ as its head. Although the structure seems confusing with phrases piled one on top of another, the interconnectedness between the head and the body cannot be missed. Embedded in the image is a two-way flow between body and head: "We must grow up . . . *into him*"; "*Christ, from whom* the whole body . . . promotes the body's growth." It is unnecessary to challenge the physiology behind this portrayal by asking how a body could grow "into" its own head, or whether it is in fact the head or the heart that "generates growth" in the rest of the body. More to the point is the fact that Christ, the head, is both the source of power and the ultimate purpose of the growth and unity of the church, his body.

The body ought to be likened to a well-oiled machine, with "each part . . . working properly." No distinction is made here between leaders and members, as all are "joined and knit together by every ligament" to form a *whole* body. Joining and knitting are synonyms that express unity and inter-dependence. A ligament is a fibrous tissue that connects one bone to the next. It is equally unnecessary to turn the picture into an allegory and view the ligaments as the leaders chosen to equip other members of the church. The overall effect is one healthy body doing what it is supposed to do.

Bringing this section to a close is the fitting reminder that growth and unity must only be nurtured "in love" (4:16), echoing Paul's earlier injunctions of "bearing with one another in love" (4:1) and "speaking the truth in love" (4:15). God's love is the power behind his truth—his good news of salvation—with the death of Jesus Christ on the cross as its ultimate demonstration. All believers, in embracing this truth, must be filled with and empowered by the same divine love both within the community of faith and in the world at large. Otherwise, just as Paul tells his spiritually gifted congregation in Corinth, without love all ministries and self-proclaimed sacrifices will amount to nothing (1 Cor 13:1-3).

Conclusion

When a text is taken out of context, the problem may not always be the theological concept, which may be sound. The problem arises when the wrong text is chosen to serve as the biblical support or justification for a theological idea or doctrine.

Our discussion of "speaking the truth in love" provides a good example of this confusion. There is nothing un-Christian about encouraging one another to tell the truth. Honesty is part of interacting with one another in a loving manner. Jesus teaches us to "let [our] word be 'Yes, Yes' or 'No, No'; for anything more than this comes from the evil one" (Matt 5:37; cf. Jas 5:12). We may refer to truth-telling as "speaking the truth in love" provided that we do not claim that we are using Ephesians 4:15 as biblical support as if to say, "See, the Bible tells us so."

As we have seen from our exploration of Ephesians 4:1-16, the meaning of "speaking the truth in love" for Paul in this context is sharing a pure gospel of salvation through the power of God's love. In addition to Matthew 5:37 and James 5:12, perhaps Ephesians 4:25, "speak the truth to our neighbors," is a more appropriate choice of biblical support for general truth-telling. In short, "speaking the truth in love" (4:15) and "speak truth to our neighbors" (4:25) are not interchangeable. We need to respect the literary context of each text, even though they come from the same chapter of the same book of the New Testament.

The threat of flawed teachings and unclear theologies continues to plague the church. How, then, do we "speak the truth in love" in the modern world? While this is not the place to discuss complicated debates, Paul's advice is worth heeding: "With all humility and gentleness, with patience, bearing with one another in love, [make] every effort to maintain the unity of the Spirit in the bond of peace" (4:2-3). These attitudes will serve us well in all intra-denominational and inter-religious dialogues as the worldwide church "grow[s] up in every way into [Christ] who is the head" (4:15). We will continue to struggle with the factions that threaten to destroy any hope of church unity. Even so, let us remember that our unity is not dependent on our ability to stay together. Instead, it is grounded in the one God, the one Lord, and the one Spirit whom we worship and serve as we speak the truth in love.

Discussion Questions

1. Have you ever felt that you needed to "speak the truth in love"? When have you used that phrase? Were you thinking about Ephesians 4:15?

2. I suggest that Paul is talking about the pure gospel message when he says to speak the truth in love. In your experience, is the church today still

"speaking the truth in love"? Consider "the church" with regard to the local church, the church in America, and the worldwide church.

3. Paul emphasizes the importance of growing in spiritual maturity as a body in order for the church to speak the truth together in love. In your community of faith, how are you helping others to grow and allowing others to help you grow?

4. What theological, intellectual, and cultural currents ("every wind of doctrine") compete with the gospel of Jesus Christ for your attention? Do you respond by avoiding them, rejecting them, or talking about them?

For Further Reading

Markus Barth, *Ephesians: Introduction, Translation, and Commentary* (Anchor Bible 34-34A; Garden City: Doubleday, 1974).

Ernest Best, *A Critical and Exegetical Commentary on Ephesians* (The International Critical Commentary; Edinburgh: T&T Clark, 1998).

Harold W. Hoehner, *Ephesians: An Exegetical Commentary* (Grand Rapids: Baker, 2002).

Andrew T. Lincoln, *Ephesians* (Word Biblical Commentary 42; Dallas: Word, 1990).

Chapter 7

Work Out Your Own Salvation

Philippians 2:12

Just $18.95 will buy you a t-shirt in a wide array of colors sporting the message "Work out your own salvation" on www.Zazzle.com. This company sells customized mugs, shirts, stationery, and even computer-generated personalized postage stamps. "Is this a Christian website?" I wondered. "What other verses might they have used in their inventory?" Not so fast. Clicking through a few more screens, I found the imprint on the back of the salvation shirt. Expecting the words ". . . with fear and trembling. —Philippians 2:12," I was both surprised and puzzled to read this instead: "Do not depend on others. —Buddha."

As it turns out, "Work out your own salvation, do not depend on others," and "Work out your own salvation with diligence" are both famous quotes of Buddha. In order to achieve salvation, or nirvana, a Buddhist must work toward it by following the Noble Eightfold Path. The goal is to rise above all attachment to earthly matters and reach a state of nothingness as the ultimate escape from the world's sufferings. Granted, this is an oversimplified statement of the Buddhist understanding of salvation. Still, attaining nirvana depends on the resolve and action of the practitioner. In other words, salvation is in the hands of the adherent. The deeper their devotion to Buddhist ideals and practices, the more merits people earn and the greater their chance of reaching nirvana. Even though in some strands of Buddhism people can get help from savior figures called bodhisattvas, at its core, Buddhism is still an individualistic religion. A Buddhist cannot depend on others, but must work diligently alone toward his or her final destiny.

From the Christian point of view, we are quick to offer a counterpoint to the Buddhist doctrine of salvation from the words of Paul: "For by grace you have been saved through faith, and this is not your own doing; it is the gift of God—not the result of works, so that no one may boast" (Eph 2:8-9). We note that in the book of Acts, Paul assures the jailer in Philippi, "Believe in the Lord Jesus, and you will be saved, you and your household" (Acts 16:31). And of course there is Paul's argument in Romans and Galatians that both Jews and Gentiles, like Abraham, are justified by faith (Rom 3:21-26; Gal 3:6-9). These Scriptures reflect the standard Christian understanding that salvation is God's free gift. In response, we can do nothing other than freely receive. By our own efforts, we Christians cannot buy admission tickets into the kingdom of God.

Since our basic belief is that salvation is pure grace, when we read Philippians 2:12 ("Work out your own salvation with fear and trembling"), this much should be clear: the verse has nothing to do with pitting "salvation by works" against "salvation by faith." Usually, when a distinction is drawn between "salvation by works" and "salvation by faith," the concern is *initial* salvation—the point of conversion. Since Paul is writing to believers in Philippi and not preaching the gospel to nonbelievers, we are not dealing with their *initial* salvation. Paul is not contradicting himself by telling Galatian, Roman, and Ephesian Christians that they are saved by faith, and then teaching Philippian Christians to earn their way into God's kingdom by good works.

That said, one may go through the following train of thought wondering, "Can salvation in Philippians 2:12 mean *final* salvation instead? As a Christian, I consider myself saved when I accepted Jesus as my personal Savior. However, the final judgment is in the future. Is Paul urging us to 'work out [our] own salvation with fear and trembling' so that we will not lose our place at the end because of spiritual complacency and a lack of witness? Look at the parable of the sheep and the goats (Matt 25:31-46). When Jesus returns I do not want to be identified as one of the goats! Perhaps, on account of my works—however works are to be defined—I will not forfeit my eternal inheritance!"

Many Christians today think of salvation in three stages that we can label justification (the point when we choose to follow Jesus), sanctification (the time when we mature in our faith journeys throughout our lifetimes), and glorification (the moment when we enter into eternal joy at Jesus' second coming). Within this framework, Paul's "working out your own salvation" refers specifically to sanctification. If it does refer to the second stage of salvation, why should we navigate this process of Christian growth with fear and trembling? Is it because there's a chance we will not make it to the third stage of glorification if we do not work hard enough? How much "working out" is enough? Or is "fear and trembling" a dramatic way of saying we must take sanctification seriously because of its eternal results? These questions show that the way we interpret Paul's words depends on the doctrinal ideas we bring to the text. We should try to let the text speak for itself as part of a larger segment in Paul's letter to a specific church. Instead, we sometimes highlight a single verse (or even just a phrase) and cover it with our general understanding of salvation so that it fits our viewpoint.

There is more to the short phrase, "work out your own salvation with fear and trembling," than meets the eye. On the surface, each segment of the verse—"work out," "your own," "salvation," "with fear and trembling"— seems easy to explain because it sounds familiar. But familiarity does not always mean clarity. It gets complicated when we ask probing questions like these: What do we mean by working out? What would be the evidence of this work? To what does Paul's "salvation" refer? Does he mean the moment of conversion or eternal salvation? Alternatively, is he dealing with a state of being and its implications? Do fear and trembling mean fright or reverence? Before whom should we display such attitudes?

When a familiar verse suddenly looks less familiar, it is a good sign. We need to be able to see Scripture afresh and ask ourselves, "Does what I think this means match its context? Have I ever paid close attention to the context?" Many sermons and reflections have focused only on Philippians 2:12, or at most on verses 12 and 13, without any mention of the flow of Paul's thought leading up to the verse and following it. We need to consider this verse against a broader backdrop that involves a much longer teaching section from Philippians 1:27 to 2:18. Only then can we appreciate the emphasis Paul places on the shared life of the Philippians as he addresses matters of unity, humility, obedience, and even salvation itself.

Is Philippians 2:12 about the sanctification of Christians, the maturing of their faith during life on earth? Yes, but it is more complex than that. On the one hand, "working out your own salvation" concerns the way in which every Christian in Philippi ought to live from now until the day of Christ. On the other hand, it is more than an individual's path toward his or her final salvation. Every Philippian Christian is accountable to the community of faith of which he or she is part. From this communal perspective, salvation is a joint affair that takes for granted the unity of the church as well as its outer witness to the world.

Philippi, the Philippian Church, and Paul's Letter to the Philippians

Situated along the Via Egnatia in Macedonia near the northeastern coast of Greece, Philippi's claim to fame at the time of the first century was its status as a Roman military outpost and provincial colony. Historically, it was at Philippi that Mark Antony and Octavian defeated the armies of Brutus and Cassius, the assassins of Julius Caesar, in 42 BC. Populated with military veterans, the city was Roman in every way from its plan and architecture to the clothing of its inhabitants. Philippians were governed under Roman law and carried Roman citizenship. This was a coveted status that came with property rights and special civic privileges.

Philippi was by far the most Latinized of the cities Paul visited on his missionary journeys. Paul founded the Philippian church around AD 49 to 52. The congregation was primarily made up of Gentile converts, since the Jewish population in the city was small. The book of Acts recounts the drama of Paul's visit to Philippi, beginning with the conversion of Lydia, his own arrest, and the later conversion of the jailer and his household (Acts 16:11-40). Although the Christians at Philippi faced opposition after Paul left, they held firm to their faith and supported him with their limited resources (4:10-16). As a result, there were close ties between Paul and his friends in this city (1:3-8; 2:17-24; 4:1). The strength of their friendship shows in this letter filled with echoes of joy, encouragement, and solidarity.

Paul wrote to the Philippians probably from Ephesus, where he was in jail awaiting trial. At that time, convicted criminals were not sentenced to a prison term as a form of punishment. Instead, prison was a holding place between arrest and trial. Paul was locked up to ensure that he would be present to stand trial, the result of which could be execution, exile, or freedom. Under such circumstances, it is not surprising that Paul mused on matters of life and death: "For to me, living is Christ and dying is gain" (1:21). He also maintained confidence that through the prayers of his friends he would be released from prison and cleared of the charge against him (1:19).

Aside from Paul's personal circumstances, one of the main purposes of his letter was to thank the Philippians for sending Epaphroditus to him with yet another gift (2:25-30; 4:10-16). Reflecting on his own imprisonment and the threats the Philippians faced, Paul advised the church on how to deal with their challenging realities. He warned them against various groups of opponents (1:28; 3:2, 18-19) and redirected them to view their suffering for Jesus as a privilege and a cause for rejoicing (1:29-30; 2:17-18; 4:4-7).

Unity in the Church

After a typical opening greeting and prayer, an update on his imprisonment, and personal reflections (1:1-26), Paul launches into a long teaching section (1:27 to 2:18) that revolves around the theme of unity. Since our target phrase, "work out your own salvation with fear and trembling," is in this portion of the letter, it is necessary for us to trace the flow of Paul's thought. I find four sub-themes here.

First, *unity is crucial in times of persecution* (1:27-30). Paul's opening statement is broad: "Only live your life (*politeuesthe*) in a manner worthy of the gospel of Christ" (1:27a). The Greek verb *politeuesthe* can also be translated as "live out your citizenship." Because the Philippians are proud of their Roman citizenship, Paul reminds them that "[their] citizenship (*politeuma*) is in heaven" (3:20). Their loyalties must no longer be to Caesar, but to Christ, their risen Lord and Savior. They are no longer soldiers in the Roman army, but now are called to "[stand] firm in one spirit, striving side by side with one mind for the faith of the gospel" (1:28), to fight against those who oppose their newfound faith in Jesus. Of all people, veteran warriors should understand how important oneness in mind and spirit is on the battleground. Moreover, if they worship a persecuted Savior and are taught by a persecuted founder, why should they expect their lot to be any different? Paul urges the Philippians to view their suffering as a way of sharing in the struggles of Paul and, in part, in those of Jesus as well (1:29-30).

Second, *humility nurtures unity* (2:1-4). The Philippians are loving and generous toward Paul, but they need to treat one another with the same affection. While Paul affirms that the Philippians are firmly grounded in their salvation, experiencing the love of Christ and the fellowship of the Spirit (2:1), he calls for unity among them in a fourfold repetition: "Be of the same mind, having the same love, being in full accord and of one mind" (2:2). Oneness means operating with a shared purpose and bond of love in Christ. Instead of selfish ambition, conceit, and self-interest, Paul promotes humility and putting others' interests before one's own (2:3-4). Here Paul is not talking about false humility and forgetting the self, but about relinquishing one's sense of entitlement for the good of others. This mutual consideration will foster unity within the church.

Third, *the best example of humility is Jesus himself* (2:5-11). When Paul writes, "Let the same mind be in you that was in Christ Jesus" (2:5), he is obviously not expecting them to have a divine mind, but he wants the congregation to adopt the attitude with which Jesus lived his life and went to the cross. The Christ hymn that follows recounts the incarnation of Jesus through his self-giving death to his exaltation by God. Jesus showed what it means not to look out for one's own interests. He "did not regard equality with God as something to be exploited," but "emptied himself," "humbled himself and became obedient to the point of death—even death on a cross" (2:6-8). Although Jesus' saving death is unique, his followers can certainly try to imitate his humility and obedience. These two qualities link the Christ hymn to the earlier call for unity in 2:1-4 and the later call for action in 2:12-18. Just as Jesus humbled himself, the Philippians are to give priority to others in humility (2:3, 8). Likewise, just as Jesus' obedience to God led him to the cross, the Philippians' obedience should support their commitment to "work out their own salvation with fear and trembling" (2:8, 12).

Fourth, *unity in the church has internal and external effects* (2:12-18). After the Christ hymn, Paul goes back to instructing. We will look at this segment in detail as we unpack the meaning of the phrase, "work out your own salvation with fear and trembling." For now, we simply note that in this subsection Paul addresses unity by bringing the world and himself into the picture. In a larger society fragmented by self-promoting gains, a Christian community united in love and purpose will draw attention to the gospel. This community will also do Paul proud on the day of Christ when everything he has invested turns out to be worth the effort.

Overall, Paul is concerned about church unity in this teaching section (1:27 to 2:18)—the need for unity, the type of humility that brings unity, the model of humility, and the far-reaching effects of unity. Because of his concern for the corporate life of the Philippians, our reading of "work out your own salvation with fear and trembling" must relate to this theme of unity. Any individualistic interpretation of salvation is secondary under this corporate focus.

Work Out Your Own Salvation

After the Christ hymn of 2:6-11, Paul resumes the urgent tone he has used since 1:27. It is as though he felt the need to jump-start the discussion again in case his readers had forgotten what came before the poetry. The next two verses, 2:12-13, are remarkably similar to 1:27-28:

> Only live your life in a manner worthy of the gospel of Christ, so that, whether I come and see you or am absent and hear about you, I will know that you are standing firm in one spirit, striving side by side with one mind from the faith of the gospel, and are in no way intimidated by your

opponents. For them this is evidence of their destruction, but of your salvation. And this is God's doing. (1:27-28)

Therefore, my beloved, just as you have always obeyed, not only in my presence, but much more now in my absence, work out your salvation with fear and trembling; for it is God who is at work in you, enabling you both to will and to work for his good pleasure. (2:12-13)

Reading the two passages alongside each other, we note five common elements. First, the Philippians are to carry out Paul's orders regardless of whether he is present with them to supervise or encourage them, or whether he is absent from them as he is now. Second, salvation is mentioned. In chapter 1, the salvation of the Philippians is set over against the destruction of their enemies, whereas in chapter 2 they are told to work out their salvation. Third, there is an element of fear. In chapter 1, Paul speaks of fear caused by intimidating opponents. In chapter 2, fear and trembling refer to an attitude the Philippians are to adopt as they work out their salvation. Fourth, the imperatives "live your life" and "work out your salvation" both suggest ongoing practices over the long haul. Fifth, God is in control and actively involved in the Philippians' formation.

These similarities are striking. If indeed Paul is repeating some of his earlier thoughts in 2:12-13 before moving on to more specific instructions in verse 14, then 1:27-28 may shed light on 2:12-13. Perhaps "work out your own salvation in fear and trembling" and "live your life in a manner worthy of the gospel of Christ" interpret each other. And if, according to 1:27-28, a life worthy of the gospel includes believers uniting to fight for the gospel, then "work out your own salvation" in 2:12 might also be interpreted as something believers do together and not in isolation.

Except for the term for salvation (*tēn sōtērian*), the other words in the phrase "work out your own salvation (*tēn heautōn sōtērian katergazesthe*)" are in the plural, since Paul is writing to a congregation. The main imperative, *katergazesthe*, is in the present tense, which indicates ongoing action in the Greek. Hence Paul's instructions may be rendered as "keep working out your own salvation" or "continuously work out your own salvation." Even though the most common English translation of *katergazesthe* is "work *out*," there is no preposition following the Greek verb *katergazesthe*. The point is not the difference between "working out" and "working at," "working for" or "working toward." Rather, *katergazesthe* carries the sense of accomplishing, doing, producing, or bringing about something. In his other letters, Paul uses this verb to say that "suffering *produces* endurance" (Rom 5:3) or "worldly grief *produces* death" (2 Cor 7:10). But "produce" would be an awkward translation here in Philippians 2:12. "Work out your own salvation" sounds less problematic than "produce your own salvation" or "accomplish your own salvation." Even though "work out your own salvation" still sounds vague, at least this translation is less likely to give the wrong impression that Paul is supporting salvation by works.

What, then, does it mean to "work something out"? It means that something is carried out over time in order to yield a desired result. Whatever that action or behavior is, the Philippians are to practice it continuously and not just once or twice. The thematic parallel in 1:27 is helpful here. "Live your life" (or "live out your citizenship") clarifies the definition of "work out your own salvation." Both refer to a way of being and acting that is consistent with the Philippians' status as people saved by the gospel of Christ. This sense of identity is to be shown in concrete attitude and action at all times with or without Paul looking over their shoulders. "Work out your own salvation" in 2:12 is about *corporate* sanctification—that is, how living in one mind and spirit is right for a vibrant, growing church in difficult circumstances. "Your *own* salvation" does not refer to a Philippian Christian's individual salvation as though it had nothing to do with everyone else's salvation. Rather, the Philippians are in this together. Each believer has a personal stake in a salvation that is shared and experienced by all.

At this point we will stay with the general understanding of "working out your own salvation" as sanctification *in the corporate sense*. In a few verses Paul will lay out what this "working out" means in more specific terms. Meanwhile, in order to explain why the Philippians are to work out this salvation "with fear and trembling," we need to jump ahead and consider verse 13 before returning to the rest of verse 12.

Paul gives the driving force for working out one's salvation: ". . . God is the one who is at work (*ho energōn*) in you, both to will and to work (*energein*) for his good pleasure" (2:13). The implication of the Greek verb *energeō* is generative; something is accomplished as a result of the "energizing." Even though the believers are working out their salvation, the source of the empowerment is God. Grammatically, "in you (*en hymin*)" may also be rendered "among you." It is not necessary to decide between "in" and "among" since the pronoun "you" is plural (i.e., "you all"). Without God's enabling of the whole group, the Philippians will not even have the resolve to "work out their own salvation," let alone the action to show for it. Hence

Paul rightly takes himself out of the equation. It should not matter whether he is present among the Philippians or not. Their potential for spiritual progress comes from God's direct empowerment, not his.

And God enables "for his good pleasure." Like a caring parent, God is pleased to prepare his children so that they may do what is good for them and bring God joy in the process. Paul encourages the Philippians at the beginning of the letter: "I am confident of this, that the one who began a good work among you will bring it to completion by the day of Jesus Christ" (1:6). Not only does God set in motion the means for the Philippians to live out or work out their salvation, but God will also see them through to the end.

With empowerment comes accountability. The Philippians are not to treat their divine gift lightly but "with fear and trembling." Fear and trembling form a "hendiadys," a figure of speech in which two similar concepts are linked together for added effect. In the Old Testament, fear and trembling are used to describe one's disposition before God, when awe and reverence go together with fright and faintheartedness (cf. Exod 15:16; Deut 2:25; Isa 19:16). God is fearsome because he is sovereign and worthy of respect. Thus it makes sense for Paul to exhort the believers to work out their salvation with fear and trembling. Surely the fear is not a cowering fear, for God is at work in them with kind intentions. But because the power comes from God, it must be properly honored and appropriated with due care. Fortunately, the Philippians are already headed in the right direction. They have a track record of consistent obedience, for Paul writes, "Just as you have always obeyed, not only in my presence, but much more now in my absence" (2:12). With Paul in prison and the Philippians facing persecution, the challenge to remain obedient is greater and so is the need to stand firm. By urging the Philippians to work out their salvation, Paul essentially reminds them to remain obedient in all they do.

Summarizing the various pieces of our discussion thus far, I suggest that a theocentric and corporate reading of 2:12-13 best fits the flow of Paul's thought and the circumstances faced by the Philippian church. "Work out your own salvation in fear and trembling" is similar to "live out your citizenship in a manner worthy of the gospel of Christ." These imperatives require the entire congregation to come together in one mind and spirit. And because this is an area of struggle for the Philippian church (cf. 4:2), Paul further assures them that God will prepare and enable them to live in unity, as long as they respond in obedience and reverence.

Before we move on to the rest of the teaching segment and its connection to the above interpretation, I would like to comment on other options for understanding 2:12-13. These options show the grammatical uncertainties in the Greek that may not be reflected in most English translations available to us today.

Broadly speaking, in Greek literature, the use of the noun "salvation (*sōteria*)" and the verb "to save (*sōzō*)" extends beyond the biblical sense of God's eternal salvation to mean general health or wholeness. There are places in the New Testament where *sōteria* and *sōzō* carry this nonreligious meaning. For example, before healing the man with the withered hand, Jesus asks his opponents whether it is lawful "to do good or to do harm on the Sabbath, to save (*sōsai*) life or to kill" (Mark 3:4). In this context, "to save life" means to restore the man to physical wholeness. In the book of Acts, Peter defends his healing of a lame beggar he describes as "someone who was sick and . . . has been healed (*sesōtai*)" (Acts 4:9). Again, physical healing is in view here, even though both of the men healed in these two examples can end up becoming followers of Jesus and receive eternal salvation as well. If this nonreligious meaning of *sōteria* is applied to Philippians 2:12, then Paul is understood to have asked the believers to do whatever it takes to restore their communal well-being, which is currently threatened by their bickering. Salvation then is almost equated with unity.

Following this train of thought, the argument maintains that the phrase, "with fear and trembling," should not be understood as a posture before God, but an attitude toward fellow human beings. To justify this reading, parts of Paul's other writings are brought in. For example, Paul uses "fear and trembling" to convey a sense of respect and honor. He describes the welcome given to Titus by the Corinthians as one offered "with fear and trembling" (2 Cor 7:15). In Ephesians, Paul exhorts Christian slaves to obey their earthly masters "with fear and trembling in singleness of heart as [they] obey Christ" (Eph 6:5), again keeping the interaction among humans. Along these lines, a consistent reading of the entire command would argue that Paul is asking the Philippians to work toward wholeness and unity by showing respect to one another.

A third interpretive move that feeds into this emphasis on unity may be found at the end of verse 13. Instead of "for his good pleasure," the prepositional phrase *hyper tēs eudokias* is translated "for goodwill toward others." This switch from God's good pleasure to the Philippians' goodwill is acceptable because there is no possessive pronoun in the Greek before the word *eudokias* to indicate whose goodwill or good pleasure it ought to be. This makes both renderings grammatically permissible. Moreover, since Paul has already spoken of Christian preachers proclaiming Christ out of goodwill (*di' eudokian*) in 1:15, should we not expect him to use the word in the same sense further along in the same letter?

The effect of these three alternate readings is to keep 2:12-13 within the confines of the issue of church unity. This is an area in which the Philippians definitely need to improve. By highlighting what the Philippians ought to do or be for one another—show respect and goodwill—the emphasis on God is somewhat lessened. Indeed, there is evidence in Paul's writings where he uses these Greek words in this manner. Together they create an even closer link between 2:12-13 and the key themes of unity and humility in the entire section of 1:27 to 2:18. The biggest compromise in adopting these alternate translations, however, is to let go of the traditional biblical understanding of salvation and give preference to a nonreligious meaning for *sōteria*. In light of Paul's concern in this letter over how the Philippians will fare on the day of Christ (Phil 1:6, 10; 2:16), it is difficult to imagine that he did not have eternal salvation in mind.

How then do we choose between these options for interpreting "work out your own salvation with fear and trembling"? At least the "group sanctification" interpretation and the "communal health" interpretation are not at odds with each other. One might suggest combining the two. This assumes that Paul expects the Philippians to get both levels of meanings, from the general to the specific, from focusing on God to focusing on one another. While this is always a possibility, it seems unlikely that Paul would pack three ambiguities into one sentence. Rather than insist on one or the other, perhaps in this case it is helpful to indicate a preference, as I have done for the "group sanctification" interpretation. I present the "communal health" interpretation as a means of enhancing the text for our learning.

Either way, we ought to be able to support our conclusion with literary and contextual evidence. Let's not randomly pick an option that sounds good to us.

Internal Unity and External Witness

What is Paul's hope for the Philippians? His call for them to "do all things without murmuring and arguing" (2:14) parallels an earlier appeal for them to "do nothing from selfish ambition or conceit" (2:3). At present, they are acting like the Israelites in the wilderness who grumbled against God and

Moses (Exod 15–17; Num 14–17). There is no indication in the letter that the Philippians blame God or Paul for their struggles, but "murmuring and arguing" among themselves are still signs of self-interest that will lead to divisiveness.

Disunity harms the church internally and also weakens the Philippians' witness for the gospel. To reverse course, the Philippians must strive to be "blameless and innocent, children of God without blemish in the midst of a crooked and perverse generation" (2:15). The alliteration in the Greek sounds out Paul's expectations of the church: *amemptoi* (without blame), *akeraioi* (without guile), and *amōma* (without blemish). Like sacrificial animals, the Philippians are to maintain a level of moral purity that makes them presentable before God.

Once again, the failure of Israel lurks in the background of Paul's words. Moses called the Israelites "spotted children" and "a crooked and perverse generation" (Deut 32:5) because they were ungrateful and disobedient. The Philippians must not be like them; their behavior must be so exemplary that they are blameless before God. Whereas Israel of old *was* the crooked and perverse generation in Deuteronomy 32, the Philippian church lives *in the midst of* a crooked and perverse generation. As such, the negative label is now applied to the unbelieving world hostile to the gospel.

The Philippians could remain in a holy huddle, disengaged from the world. But what good is a Christian community in the midst of non-believing neighbors if it exerts no influence on them? While opposition is difficult, it is still an opportunity. Paul insists that the Philippians' behavior and unity be apparent, even to outsiders, so that they "shine as luminaries (*phainesthe hōs phōstēres*) in the world" (2:15). An allusion to Daniel's apocalyptic vision may be intended here: "And the wise shall shine as the luminaries (*phanousin hōs phōstēres*)" (Dan 12:3). Although the context in Daniel refers to the future glorification of the righteous, Paul's reminder to the Philippian Christians of their role as God's witnesses is relevant here and now. Israel, too, was supposed to be "light to the nations" (Isa 42:6), but their history was strewn with failed attempts to prove themselves blameless as children of God. Therefore, unless the Philippians take seriously the assurance that God is at work in them as they work out their salvation together, they will fare no better than Israel.

Joy in Solidarity

As Paul brings this teaching segment to a close, his tone becomes personal. Expressing his hope for the Philippians, Paul writes, "It is by your holding fast to the word of life that I can boast on the day of Christ that I did not run in vain or labor in vain" (2:16). In a different letter, Paul refers to the Corinthian congregation as his "letter of recommendation" (2 Cor 3:1-3). How the Corinthians turn out or what they become as a community reflects how well Paul has led and nurtured them in the faith. By the same token, here in Philippi, if the believers persevere in persecution and stand firm for the gospel, then Paul can be proud of them on the day of reckoning. He is not boasting about his contribution to their success, but expressing his pride and joy in them.

Paul employs two separate metaphors to emphasize his personal investment in the Philippians' growth as a church. First, he does not want to run in vain. Like an athlete, he runs with the goal that the Philippians "may be pure and blameless in the day of Jesus Christ" (1:10). Elsewhere Paul uses the image of a race to describe his work for the gospel and his care for the flock. The race entails hard work, self-discipline, and a focus on the prize that awaits him at the end (1 Cor 9:24-26). Indeed Paul knows he has run his race well (2 Tim 4:7), but the Philippians need to know that *they* serve as the "evidence" that he has done so, and they must not let Paul down.

Second, neither does Paul want to labor in vain. This image comes from his background as a tentmaker. Manual labor is tough. After toiling for a long time to prepare a piece of cloth as a tentmaker, it would be disappointing if the cloth were found unusable. In chapter 1 when Paul ponders the possibilities of life and death as an outcome of his trial, his conclusion is that staying alive is preferable for the sake of the Philippians: "To remain in the flesh is more necessary for you. Since I am convinced of this, I know that I will remain and continue with all of you for your progress and joy in the faith" (1:24-25). Even though Paul is absent from his friends, he continues to be deeply committed to them.

The depth of Paul's commitment to the Philippian church is further expressed in the next verse: "But even if I am being poured out as a libation over the sacrifice and the offering of your faith, I am glad and rejoice with all of you—and in the same way you also must be glad and rejoice with me" (2:17-18). In 2 Timothy, the same image is used to describe the many sufferings Paul has endured throughout his life for the sake of the gospel: "I am already being poured out as a libation, and the time of my departure has come" (2 Tim 4:6). This image is easily understood in both the Jewish and Greco-Roman worlds. A libation is a drink poured on the ground or on the sacrifice in honor of the one to whom the sacrifice is made, whether a deity or an ancestor. Even though Paul's life is frequently in danger in the course of his missionary work, he is probably not talking about martyrdom in this letter. He expects that he will be released (1:19, 25-26). Rather, Paul assures the Philippians that he will gladly suffer for and alongside them as they offer themselves and their faith as a sacrificial service to God. In the Old Testament, the libation, or drink offering, is not a lone offering. It usually accompanies some form of burnt offering (Num 28–29). Similarly, Paul's self-giving is linked with that of the Philippians. United in the joy of salvation, they now share the privilege of suffering as well (1:29-30).

If the Philippians are willing to treat Paul with such self-giving love, why can't they do the same for one another? If they are of one mind in their support of Paul, who is but one person, how much more will their unity as a church serve the greater purposes of God's kingdom? Indeed, the Philippians have the potential to share Paul's joy and "shine like luminaries in the world." To be truly effective for the gospel, they must get rid of their interest in outshining one another. Then they will be well on their way to working out their salvation—with fear and trembling, yes, but also for the pleasure and glory of God.

Conclusion

In the Gospel of John, Jesus warns his disciples, "Apart from me you can do nothing" (John 15:5). In his letter to the Philippians, Paul sends the same message, stated positively: "It is God who is at work in you to enable you to work out your own salvation with fear and trembling." If we read Philippians 2:12 and remember only the second half of the sentence, we miss the promise that gives encouragement and motivation. Worse, we then read "work out your own salvation" in the singular and put all the responsibility on ourselves. We become so worried about what we are supposed to do for God that we forget that God initiates our desire to be obedient in the first place. Left to our own devices, we are trapped in a cycle of defeat. No wonder the thought of "working out our own salvation" seems like an impossible task, and "with fear and trembling" becomes a debilitating self-fulfilling prophecy.

When we look around our churches today, we see how Paul's encouraging challenge to his friends in Philippi could be turned into a load of burdens. We sometimes carry a picture of God holding a clipboard in his hand, recording all that we have done for him as evidence of our sanctification, as though there is a quota to meet before we die. When I catch myself thinking this way, I wonder where I have misplaced God's grace and bought into Buddha's teaching: "Work out your own salvation. Do not depend on others." We speak of salvation by grace and not by works, but we subscribe to sanctification by works and not by grace. Our performance-driven mindset clouds our ability to recognize how we came to faith in Jesus and how we now live as followers of Jesus. Surely good works are natural expressions of a transformed life in Christ, but if we count on them as deposits in a "spiritual account" that qualifies us for a place in eternity, then we have not yet come to grips with the full extent of our powerlessness. Paul's words remind us that God is the empowering source of our sanctification, and the community of faith provides the training ground for it. Both are available to us if we choose not to make the journey alone. For starters, all it takes is a simple prayer and a dab of humility.

Discussion Questions

1. If you are a Christian, have you ever doubted your eternal salvation? If so, what triggered your doubt?

2. Paul speaks in general terms: "work out your salvation with fear and trembling," "live your life in a manner worthy of the gospel of Christ." Think about your own journey of faith, both as an individual and as a member of the corporate body of Christ. On what specific areas do you think God is calling you to focus at this time? How can you seek trusted help from fellow Christians to move you along in the process?

3. Paul keeps the Philippian Christians accountable even though he is unable to be with them at all times. Do you have someone to keep you accountable in your journey of faith? Do you keep someone else accountable? What benefit do you see in such a relationship?

For Further Reading

Gordon D. Fee, *Paul's Letter to the Philippians* (New International Commentary on the New Testament; Grand Rapids: Eerdmans, 1995).

Stephen E. Fowl, *Philippians* (The Two Horizons New Testament Commentary; Grand Rapids: Eerdmans, 2005).

Paul Hartog, "'Work out Your Salvation': Conduct 'Worthy of the Gospel' in a Communal Context," *Themelios* 33 (2008): 19–33, http://thegospelcoalition.org/publications/33-2/work-out-your-salvation-conduct-worthy-of-the-gospel-in-a-communal-context.

Peter T. O'Brien, *The Epistle to the Philippians: A Commentary on the Greek Text* (Grand Rapids: Eerdmans, 1991).

John Reumann, *Philippians: A New Translation with Introduction and Commentary* (Anchor Yale Bible 33B; New Haven: Yale University Press, 2008).

Chapter 8

Lukewarm Christians and Jesus at the Door

Revelation 3:16, 20

Scenario number one: Volunteer Recruitment Sunday. After the New Testament reading from Revelation 3:14-22, a deacon walks to the podium and promotes the ministries of the church: "The insert in your bulletin lists the areas where the church needs your help: babysitting, ushering, visiting the elderly, and cooking. Please do not let 5 percent of the members do 85 percent of the work. The Scripture we just read warns us not to be pew-warmers. Jesus would rather us be hot and fervent, or even cold and hostile, but never lukewarm. Show your love for God by filling out the form and dropping it in the offering plate!"

Scenario number two: evangelism training session. After handing out gospel tracts, the leader prepares his team for evangelism at the shopping mall: "Support your points with Bible verses. Show the universality of human sinfulness by citing Romans 3:23: 'All have sinned and fall short of the glory of God.' For the consequences of sin, use Romans 6:23: 'The wages of sin is death.' When you get to the invitation, quote Jesus in Revelation 3:20: 'I am standing at the door, knocking.' If they are willing to open the door of their hearts to Jesus, pray with them to accept Jesus as their personal Lord and Savior. Remember, you are competing with Macy's. There is no time to look up the verses. Memorize them before you go."

While these scenarios are caricatures, they are familiar. Both the deacon and the team leader use excerpts from the letter to the church in Laodicea, the last of the seven letters to the churches in Asia Minor in Revelation 2 and 3. The deacon understands lukewarm Christians as lazy pew-warmers, and the team leader identifies conversion with opening the door of one's heart to Jesus. Encouraging the congregation to participate in church ministries and assuring nonbelievers that Jesus desires a personal relationship with them are important aspects of Christian discipleship and evangelism. But do pew-warming churchgoers and the hearts of nonbelievers reflect the concerns of John when he penned these words on the island of Patmos?

When the letter to the church of Laodicea is taken as a complete literary unit, the use of those verses in the scenarios I described is suspect. First, John addresses Christians, so Jesus is standing at the door of believers, not nonbelievers. Second, if hot, cold, and lukewarm indicate the recipients' spiritual temperature, Jesus' wish for them to be either cold or hot implies that the rejection of Jesus (coldness) is preferred to the half-hearted commitment of spiritually immature believers (lukewarmness). Surely some measure of faith is better than outright unbelief. Like the well-meaning deacon and team leader in our examples, we, too, may have assigned a meaning to this text that is foreign to its contexts. In our eagerness to find a quotation that gives our words scriptural authority, we sometimes violate the integrity of the text. In spite of our good intentions, we obscure the message the author wanted to convey and substitute it with something else.

These verses in Revelation 3:14-22 are especially prone to misinterpretation. "Hot," "cold," and "door" are common words for describing interpersonal relationships. Giving someone a warm embrace or a cold shoulder is a means of expressing emotional distance. The opening or closing of the door of one's heart signals reception or rejection. The lyrics found in popular music today reflect this usage. Paula Cole has a song by the title "Heart Door." The refrain of a song by Hank Williams, Jr., reads, "Why can't I free your doubtful mind and melt your cold, cold heart?" Pete Townsend sings, "Let my love open the door to your heart, I have the only key to your heart." These examples are easily multiplied. The same idea is also found in hymns, such as, "Open my eyes that I may see glimpses of truth Thou hast for me. . . . Open my heart and let me prepare love with Thy children thus to share." Whether we want them to or not, these patterns and associations become the filter through which we process the words "hot," "cold," and "door" when we read this passage in Revelation. Although the word "heart" is never mentioned in the letter to the Laodiceans, we see the word "door" and register "door of the heart." We read, "I wish you were either cold or hot" (3:15) and think to ourselves, "Jesus wants us to take a clear stance, either say no to him or love him fervently. Anything in between is indecisive and unacceptable." But the point is, did the Laodicean Christians have the same thoughts when they first heard the letter read two millennia ago?

The book of Revelation was written around the last decade of the first century during the reign of the Roman emperor Domitian. Like the other six churches in this series of letters, the Laodicean church had its own historical, geographical, cultural, and congregational particularities. Let's try to suspend what we naturally think this text means. We are reminded at the end of the letter, "Let anyone who has an ear listen to what the Spirit is saying to the churches" (3:22). Attentive listening is helpful for proper understanding. Before us is an ancient letter full of images of local color and allusions that the first-century readers would have understood. But being far removed from them in time, distance, culture, and language, we need to study their historical context. The task of biblical interpretation involves hearing the message alongside the Laodiceans before we hear it again in our personal, ministerial, and congregational contexts.

Laodicea, the City and Its Church

Laodicea was situated in the Lycus river valley in the southwestern part of the province of Phrygia. Founded by the Seleucid king Antiochus II in the third century BC, the city had been under Roman rule since 133 BC. It soon rose to prominence, thanks to two trade routes running through it. The first extended from Ephesus on the western shore of Asia Minor to the Aegean Sea in the east, and the second from Pergamum in the north to the Mediterranean in the south. Laodicea not only developed into a major banking and judicial center of the Lycus Valley but also had a famous medical school that specialized in ophthalmology and a thriving textile industry of fine wool. Laodicea was prosperous and had no trouble making it known; its coinage frequently featured the image of a cornucopia.

Ironically, this success put its relationship with Rome on a delicate balance. On the one hand, favor with the emperor worked toward the city's economic growth. Imperial support meant well-maintained infrastructure that was crucial to trade and commerce. On the other hand, its wealth made it a target of heavy taxation and abuse by the Romans. Even so, Laodicea continued to do well and its population grew.

With expansion, the natural challenges of Laodicea became more acute. First, the entire region was volcanically active and prone to earthquakes. Several large earthquakes in the city's history required it to be rebuilt. Second, the city lacked a good natural source of water. With the increase in population, it had to bring in water by means of an aqueduct. These municipal projects were costly. Fortunately, the city was never in short supply of rich local benefactors.

The church in Laodicea comprised both Jewish and Gentile believers. This congregation, together with the one in Hieropolis six miles to the north and another in Colossae eleven miles to the east, formed a cluster of interrelated churches (Col 2:1; 4:13, 15-16). Since it might have been Epaphras, Paul's coworker, who founded the church in Colossae (Col 1:7), perhaps the same applied to Laodicea as well.

Addressing the Laodicean church is Jesus, "the Amen, the faithful and true witness, the beginning of God's creation" (3:14). In the Hebrew text of Isaiah, Yahweh is called the "God of Amen" (Isa 65:16), a designation later translated as "God of truth" (NIV, RSV, NKJV) or "God of faithfulness" (NRSV). Here in Revelation these same attributes describe Jesus, whose name is "Faithful and True" (19:11). He is also "the faithful witness" who rules over the earth (1:5). Jesus is supreme because of his work in creation. He is the beginning of God's creation, both in the temporal and causal sense. As Paul states in his letter to the Colossians, "In [the Son] all things in heaven and on earth were created . . . all things have been created through him and for him" (Col 1:16). These designations for Jesus signal the message of the letter: the Laodicean church is responsible before the faithful and true witness because its own witness falls short of these marks.

Indictment and Diagnosis

The indictment against the congregation is expressed in metaphorical terms: "I know your works, that you are neither cold nor hot. I wish that you were either cold or hot" (3:15). In this verse, the transition between "your works" and "you" is seamless, implying that the church's works reflect the congregation behind them. The works of the church are supposed to give evidence to its impact on the city. Jesus describes this church as "neither cold nor hot" while wishing that it were at least one or the other. The report is grim. The Laodicean church misses the mark on both scores.

The clue to the referents of these extreme temperatures is found in the next verse: "So, because you are lukewarm, and neither cold nor hot, I am about to spit you out of my mouth" (3:16). Although water is not mentioned, the image of something coming from a person's mouth implies that hot, cold, and lukewarm are all descriptions of water. In fact, these adjectives match the waters of Hieropolis, Colossae, and Laodicea exactly. The original readers would have thought not about their spiritual temperature but about the water supply of their city as compared to those of their close neighbors.

Across the valley, Hieropolis loomed six miles to the north in full view of Laodicea. Hot water from underground springs bubbled to the surface of the plateau and cascaded down to the valley below in gullied channels. The resulting formation was a wall of white, calcified cliffs, three hundred feet deep and about a mile wide. The water was rich in mineral content and recognized for its healing properties. The abundance of healing shrines there had propelled Hieropolis into a regional health center. While drinkable, the water in the hot springs did not taste particularly good. The impurities made it more useful for washing or irrigation than for drinking. For better tasting water, one had to draw from the natural springs of Colossae. This city, unlike Laodicea, had a perennial stream of cold running water, a scarcity in the surrounding area. So when Jesus says the Laodicean church is "neither cold nor hot," he is comparing it to Laodicea's water supply, which is neither cold like the refreshing streams of Colossae nor hot like the medicinal springs of Hieropolis.

But how did the water at Laodicea get to be that way, if it was only two miles from the Lycus River? The Lycus River was not a reliable source of water for Laodicea. The water was clouded with impurities and the river sometimes dried up during the summer. As the need for water in Laodicea grew, an aqueduct was built to bring in water from the outside. Today, among the ruins of Laodicea are remains of doubly insulated hollow stone pipes that extend in the direction of modern-day Denizli. Limestone deposits inside these pipes suggest that the aqueduct channeled water from a hot spring somewhere to the south of the city. For whatever reason, the pipes were not connected to the cold springs of Colossae. By the time the hot water in the aqueduct reached Laodicea, it had already cooled to a lukewarm temperature. Had the water still been piping hot, the Laodiceans could have taken advantage of its medicinal quality. Had the cool waters of Colossae been tapped instead, they would have enjoyed better tasting water. Instead, the solution the Laodiceans devised for their problem turned out to be neither here nor there, just like the water they ended up getting, which was neither hot nor cold.

The indictment against Laodicea, therefore, is that it resembles neither the hot springs of Hieropolis nor the cool springs of Colossae. Whether hot or cold, the waters of Hieropolis and Colossae both fulfill their distinctive functions and are appreciated. Effective functionality is the way to understand the metaphor. Temperature is only relevant in relation to the way in which the water is deemed useful. It should be noted that Jesus is not comparing three churches but the water supplies of three cities. The works of the churches of Hieropolis and Colossae are not under examination, even though these congregations know one another and circulate apostolic letters between them. In short, the stress lies not on Laodicea's lukewarm water in and of itself, but that it is neither effectively hot for the healing of ailments nor effectively cold for the quenching of thirst.

Therefore, Jesus' words to the Laodicean church, "I know your works," essentially mean, "I know the ineffectiveness of your works because you are ineffective." He does not specify what is ineffective or the specific works he has in mind. We may ask, "What about the spiritual temperature of the Laodicean Christians? Isn't effectiveness a measure of enthusiasm? Is it possible for a church to be fervent yet at the same time ineffective in witnessing?" With regard to these questions, the text is silent, except for the frightful possibility of being rejected by Jesus.

While the Greek infinitive *emesai* is usually rendered "to spit" in most English versions, "to vomit" is a valid translation. The picture of Jesus vomiting his church out of his mouth highlights the seriousness of the offense. A similar image is found in the Old Testament, in which the land is said to "vomit out its inhabitants" should the Israelites ignore God's commandments and follow the ways of the Canaanites (Lev 18:25, 28; 20:22). The bottom line is that if the church has nothing healing or life-giving to benefit its contemporary culture, its existence will make no difference to Jesus or to the city of Laodicea.

Before any corrective measures can take place, the congregation must take an honest look at its true condition. The words of the Laodicean Christians show their false sense of security: "I am rich, I have prospered, and I need nothing" (3:17). These bold claims reflect the attitude not only of the church but of the city as a whole. To the wealthy citizens of Laodicea, the idea of building a legacy involved donating large sums toward public works. Monuments and inscriptions bearing their names adorned the public space for all to see. Although Laodicea received imperial help after the earthquake of AD 14, it turned down a similar offer when another earthquake struck in AD 60. The inhabitants showed Rome that they could afford to rebuild the city with private money, and they did. Nicostratus funded a stadium with an arena that measured three hundred yards long; Pomponius Flaccus paid for the heating of the covered walkways and the piped oil to the baths. Among the archaeological remains of structures built during the decades of reconstruction is a triple-arched gate with fortified towers. This elaborate gate was a symbol of self-sufficiency and self-determination. It sent a message to Rome—at least in attitude if not in reality—that Laodicea would welcome or reject whomever it wanted.

As the ethos of the city penetrates the church, it is a short step from having no need of Rome to having no need of Jesus. This sense of complacency is not new among the people of God. In the Old Testament, Israel was bursting with self-satisfaction behind these words: "Ah, I am rich; I have gained wealth for myself. In all of my gain no offense has been found in me that would be sin" (Hos 12:8). In the Gospel of Luke, Jesus underscores the danger of self-centeredness in the parable of the rich fool (Luke 12:16-21). The rich man is not faulted for having a bumper crop. He is, however, preoccupied with saving the harvest to secure a comfortable future for himself. He neither thanks God nor thinks of being generous to his neighbors. His words are punctuated with first person pronouns. At the end of the story Jesus calls him a fool. Similarly, amid the prosperity of Laodicea the members of the church have joined ranks with the rest of the city. They have pushed Jesus out of the life of the church because he is no longer needed. Like lukewarm water that causes neither scalding nor condensation, they have not even noticed the difference.

In a tone that suggests a prophetic oracle or his own critique of the Pharisees in Matthew 23, Jesus pulls no punches with the Laodiceans: "You do not realize that you are wretched, pitiable, poor, blind, and naked" (3:17). Every word describes what the Laodiceans think they are not. One can almost imagine their protest: "How can we be poor when our banking industry is flourishing? How can we be blind when the best ophthalmologists practice at our medical school? How can we be naked when we export clothing of fine wool? Call some other city wretched and pitiable, but never the city of Laodicea!" Yet Jesus, the Amen, the faithful and true witness, renders an accurate judgment. If these Christians cannot recognize their false sense of security in the first place, they will not be able to save themselves from this condition. Deliverance must come from without, and only Jesus can bring it.

Remedy and Command

Jesus provides one remedy consisting of three parts. The Laodicean Christians are to depend on him for all their spiritual resources: "Buy from me gold refined by fire so that you may be rich; and white robes to clothe you and to keep the shame of your nakedness from being seen; and salve to anoint your eyes so that you may see" (3:18). Each item addresses one of the three symptoms—their spiritual poverty (gold), their shame (robes), and their lack of insight (salve). In the Gospels, Jesus frequently uses fig trees, vineyards, and other agricultural metaphors to which the peasants of Palestine can relate. Likewise, here he draws on images that hit home directly for the Laodiceans. The effect, full of local color and local pride, shows the contrast between what the city claims for itself and what Jesus offers.

First, Jesus offers purified gold for the Laodicean church to buy. Laodicea was the largest banking center of the region. Even the Roman pro-consul Cicero, en route to the province of Cilicia in AD 51, exchanged his currency in this city. Instead of making money off currency exchange and other financial dealings, Jesus counsels these Christians to buy from him gold refined by fire. In biblical imagery, putting precious metals through fire symbolizes either a trial that strengthens faith or cleansing that removes sin (Job 23:10; Zech 13:9; 1 Pet 6:9). Proverbs 27:21 especially speaks of being tested not by adversity but by success: "The crucible is for silver, and the furnace is for gold, so a person is tested by being praised." In this regard, the Laodiceans have failed the test. Their success has made them complacent instead of vigilant.

Second, behind Jesus' offer of white robes is an allusion to the city's booming garment industry. Although textile production could be found in many of the cities in the region, the Laodicean sheep breeders surpassed their competition by raising black sheep whose wool was superior in sheen and softness. Without the expense of dyeing, the lower cost of production yielded higher profit margins. Garments woven from this natural black wool became one of the chief exports of Laodicea. Yet in the case of this congregation, Jesus implies that wearing the elegant and expensive woolen garments of Laodicea is like wearing nothing at all. Like the emperor in Hans Christian Andersen's famous story, *The Emperor's New Clothes*, the Laodicean Christians don't realize their nakedness. The white robes of Jesus not only cover their shame but also identify them as people washed clean by his blood. Earlier in the book of Revelation, Jesus has already promised the faithful in the church of Sardis that if they persevere he will clothe them in white clothes (3:4-5). Later, the twenty-four elders (4:4), the faithful martyrs (6:11), the multitudes that come through the great tribulation (7:9-14), and the armies of heaven (19:13) are all dressed in white. If the Laodicean

Christians put on these white robes from Jesus, they will find themselves in the fine company of the saints.

Third, Jesus offers the church an eye salve to cure its blindness. In Laodicea was a famous medical school founded by Zeuxis. This school was probably related to the shrine of the Phrygian god of healing, Mēn Carus, located thirteen miles to the west of Laodicea in Attuda. Zeuxis was succeeded by Alexander Philalethes, who in turn taught Demosthenes Philalethes. These physicians represented a tradition of medical practice that went back to Herophilus of Chalcedon (330–250 BC), an accomplished ophthalmologist who pioneered the mixing of metallic salts and herbs to cure complex eye diseases. Some interpreters comment that the significance of Jesus' offer of eye salve lies in its contrast with the eye salve made of Phrygian powder developed by the physicians at Laodicea's medical school. This is likely valid, as long as we know that the evidence is circumstantial. We actually do not have any existing ancient document that specifically names Laodicea or its medical school as the producer of an eye salve made from Phrygian powder.

Some clues, however, are available from a variety of written sources. When taken together, they seem to point in that direction. The author of pseudo-Aristotle mentions the keen eyesight of the copper miners at Chalcedon, where Phrygian powder, an ingredient of eye salve, could be found. Pliny also mentions Phrygian stone, though only in association with another mineral used in medicines for the eye. In writing about treatments for the eyes and ears, Galen refers to an ear ointment from Laodicea, perhaps to highlight an obscured fact, since the medical school was already known for ophthalmology. By itself, none of these references can make the case, but together they paint a convincing picture. First, Laodicea was also located in the province of Phrygia. The Phrygian stone or powder of Chalcedon could have been readily available there. Second, since the physicians at the medical school were students of Herophilus of Chalcedon, they could have inherited a recipe for eye salve that used Phrygian powder as one of its ingredients. Third, a commercial center like Laodicea would be able to manufacture a product and make itself known for it through effective marketing. Even if we are correct on these counts, the best eye salve from the most famous medical school of the region would still prove ineffective when compared to Jesus' eye salve. Only the one who is the beginning of God's creation, who opens the eyes of the blind, can restore spiritual vision to a church gone blind.

Although Jesus' words are difficult to hear, they are meant to save his church before it is too late. Just as God disciplines Israel as a loving father would discipline his wayward child, Jesus assures the congregation of his intention: "I reprove and discipline those whom I love" (3:19; cf. Deut 8:5; Prov 3:12). God's words to the rich man in Jesus' parable can be applied to the Laodicean Christians: "You fool! This very night your life is being demanded of you. And the things you have prepared, whose will they be?" No amount of earthly goods can compare to the value of heavenly treasures (Luke 12:20-21, 32-34). Fortunately for the Laodiceans, time has not yet run out. In urging them to "be earnest and repent" (3:19), Jesus commands that they repent from their self-congratulatory attitude, focus their energy on things of lasting value, and begin bearing an effective witness for the gospel.

Divine Initiative and Promise

The picture of Jesus at the door is a vivid portrayal of divine initiative. Jesus expresses his desire to reestablish ties with his congregation: "I am standing at the door, knocking; if you hear my voice and open the door, I will come in to you and eat with you, and you with me" (3:20). The Old Testament is filled with metaphors of God reaching out to wayward Israel, whether as a husband to his wife (Hos 2:14-20), a father to his child (Jer 31:18-20), or a shepherd to his sheep (Ezek 34:11-15). By the same token, Jesus now extends himself toward a church that has lost its dependence on him. Since the Laodiceans do not even realize the extent of their complacency, unless Jesus positions himself at the door and knocks, there will not be any response on their part, let alone a meal to follow. Therefore, the interpretation of a person opening the door of one's heart to Jesus not only piles a second image on top of an existing one but also shifts the emphasis away from the grace in Jesus' action and focuses on human responsiveness. In other words, even the receptiveness of the church is a result of divine grace. Jesus knocks first, and then the Laodiceans open the door.

The door is simply the door to a house, not a person's heart. The boundary of a home defines the in-group and the out-group within the network of social relationships. Jesus presents himself as a guest who hopes to share a meal with the owner of the house. The phrase, "I will come in to you," means "I will enter the house from where I am outside to where you are inside," not "I will come *into* you" as in the notion of indwelling. This echoes his promise to his disciples shortly before he goes to the cross: "Those who love me will keep my word, and my Father will love them, and we will come to them and make our home with them" (John 14:23). In ancient Jewish and Greco-Roman culture, entering a person's home and eating together enacted a bond of trust, friendship, and communion. Jesus is commonly shown in the Gospels to be at table with a wide range of people, from sinners and tax collectors to disciples and Pharisees. His mission was inclusive. In the same way, he expresses his desire to be in fellowship and community with his church.

Because the Laodicean church previously shut him out by announcing that they needed nothing, Jesus will not force his way back in. Any hint of an unwanted intruder may bring back unpleasant memories for the Laodiceans, especially for the affluent families of the city. As earlier mentioned, the richer the city became, the more Rome took advantage of its legal and political rights. In addition to heavy taxation, some Roman officials and their staff took the power of requisite lodging to new heights when they came to Laodicea. Wealthy citizens were forced to subsidize their expenses with meals, clothing, and lodging. The richest of the city bore the brunt of the Romans' exploitation of hospitality, a value otherwise highly esteemed in the ancient Mediterranean culture. Unlike the Romans, Jesus' call for entry is not exploitative but reconciliatory. His voice should be familiar to believers (John 5:25; 18:37), who are like sheep that can distinguish between the voice of the shepherd and that of a stranger (John 10:3-5, 27). If the Laodicean Christians have not yet become hard of hearing as well, they will recognize the voice of Jesus and open the door for him.

Another loose connection may be found in a scene from the Song of Songs, in which the husband calls on his beloved, "Listen! My beloved is knocking. 'Open to me, my sister, my love, my dove, my perfect one'" (Song 5:2). While the analogy of Jesus as the bridegroom and the Laodicean church his bride may be suggestive, we should note that the story line in the Song of Songs is different from what we have here. In the Song of Songs, the woman hesitates at first, and by the time she opens the door the man is gone. This is not the case when Jesus stands at the door. He does not leave but expresses his desire for an extended, unhurried meal: "I will . . . eat with you and you with me" (3:20). The sense of peace around a table shared with Jesus probably stands in marked contrast with a wealthy citizen's urge to satisfy imposing Roman officials and quickly send them on their way.

The present table fellowship between Jesus and his church foreshadows the heavenly banquet of the Messiah and all those who belong to him. The final promise of the letter, "To the one who conquers I will give a place with me on my throne, just as I myself conquered and sat down with my Father on his throne" (3:21), echoes the words of Jesus to his disciples at the Last Supper in the Gospel of Luke: "You are those who have stood by me in my trials; and I confer on you, just as my Father has conferred on me, a kingdom, so that you may eat and drink at my table in my kingdom, and you will sit on thrones judging the twelve tribes of Israel" (Luke 22:28-30). In these two passages, the theme of the meal, signifying fellowship with Jesus, works both at the present time and at the final consummation. Those who have proven themselves faithful for the sake of Jesus will exercise true power in justice and righteousness. In fact, the next chapter gives a preview of this grand promise in the vision of the heavenly court: "Around the throne [of God] are twenty-four thrones, and seated on the thrones are twenty-four elders, dressed in white robes, with golden crowns on their heads" (4:4).

With this grand promise the letter comes to a close: "Let anyone who has an ear listen to what the Spirit is saying to the churches" (3:22). Is the church in Laodicea willing to trust the words of the true and faithful witness and respond accordingly? Will they risk the ridicule that often goes along with effective witnessing? Dare they tell the citizens of a self-sufficient and wealthy city that they, too, are wretched, pitiable, poor, blind, and naked? Will they take up the role of a welcoming host and invite Jesus again into their midst? Someday we will have the answers to these questions, provided that we, too, make it to the messianic banquet, white robes and all. In the meantime, the same challenge to the church in Laodicea is placed before our churches. Is Jesus at the table, or is he standing outside pressing on a broken doorbell?

Conclusion

The letter to the church in Laodicea is powerful. Every point is conveyed by an analogy to some local color or historical reference: its water supply, economy, industry, or relationship with Rome. Mental pictures of the aqueduct, the ornate buildings, the inscriptions on monuments, the smells and sounds of trade and commerce, and the arrival of Roman troops help make the letter come alive for modern readers.

How shocking it is for the Christians of Laodicea to realize that the way in which they feel about the lukewarm and murky water of their city is comparable to the way Jesus feels about them. Had Laodicea's water resembled the cool running streams of Colossae or the medicinal hot springs of Hieropolis, it would have fulfilled a distinct function. But it was neither hot enough to heal nor cold enough to refresh. Likewise, the church in Laodicea has become ineffective. Worse still, the people do not realize that they are on the verge of rejection by Jesus. Having relied on things that define the city and its success—banking, textile, and medicine—they have nothing to show but poverty, shame, and blindness. The road to renewal begins with getting rid of their self-satisfying attitude, inviting Jesus back into their midst, and relying on him to restore their spiritual honor, insight, and riches. Only then will these Christians find themselves eligible to receive the promise of the future—the privilege to rule with Jesus in his future kingdom.

Complacency leads to the loss of self-awareness, and the loss of self-awareness leads to spiritual apathy. This message is important. Let's not use it out of context, as in the two scenarios introduced at the beginning of this chapter. To motivate a congregation to get involved in the church's ministries, one might look instead to the division of labor and prayerful collaboration in the early church (Acts 6:1-6). To encourage a nonbeliever to respond positively to the good news of salvation, observe the way in which Jesus interacts with the woman at the well in John 4 or the man by the pool of Bethesda in John 5. Otherwise, let Revelation 3:14-22 speak as a unit. If we don't, we miss the warning of Jesus and the call to repentance. Let anyone, then and now, who has an ear listen to what the Spirit is saying to the churches.

Discussion Questions

1. Imagine that you know nothing about the ancient city of Laodicea. What can you say about the message of the letter from a plain or surface reading of it?

2. How does knowledge of the local characteristics of Laodicea help you understand the letter? Which image is especially vivid for you and why?

3. Is complacency the same as laziness? How is complacency related to self-sufficiency and pride?

4. Is it possible for a church to be active and ineffective at the same time? In what way is this reflected in individual lives?

5. Do you sometimes sense a tension between wanting to let Jesus in while secretly also wanting to keep him out? Why do you feel this way?

6. What does being a faithful and true witness look like for you and your church? What blurs the line between compromising with the world's standards and staying relevant to contemporary culture?

For Further Reading

David Aune, *Revelation 1–5* (Word Biblical Commentary 52A; Dallas: Word, 1997).

G. K. Beale, *The Book of Revelation* (The New International Greek Testament Commentary; Grand Rapids: Eerdmans, 1999).

Colin J. Hemer, *The Letters to the Seven Churches of Asia in Their Local Setting* (Sheffield: JSOT Press, 1986).

Craig R. Koester, "The Message to Laodicea and the Problem of Its Local Context: A Study of the Imagery in Revelation 3.14-22," *New Testament Study* 49 (2003): 407–24.

Made in the USA
Monee, IL
07 July 2026

56551601R00085